# CBT WORKBOOK FOR CHILDREN AND ADOLESCENT

Over 40 fun exercises with positive affirmations to empower young minds overcome anxiety, build resilience and emotional wellbeing

# John H. Eric

# Table of Contents

# DEDICATION

Dear, the young reader, holding this book in your hands. This book is dedicated to your incredible potential, your unique strengths, and the amazing journey of self-discovery you're embarking on. It's dedicated to your courage to explore your inner world, your willingness to learn and grow, and your inherent capacity for resilience and joy. May this book serve as a trusted companion, a source of support and guidance, and a reminder that you are capable of incredible things. Know that you are not alone, that your feelings matter, and that you have the power to shape your own happiness and well-being. This book is for you, with hope and belief in all that you are and all that you will become.

# ACKNOWLEDGEMENT

To you, the reader, thank you. Thank you for picking up this book and choosing to embark on this journey of self-discovery. Writing this book has been a privilege, but it's your willingness to engage with the material, to reflect on your experiences, and to put these ideas into practice that will truly bring these pages to life. Your courage to explore your inner world, your commitment to personal growth, and your openness to change are what make this work meaningful. It is your journey, your story, and your potential that inspired every word. I am deeply grateful for the opportunity to be a small part of your path, and I sincerely hope that this book serves as a helpful companion as you continue to learn, grow, and flourish. May your journey be filled with self-compassion, resilience, and joy.

# INTRODUCTION

Have you ever had the feeling that your mind is acting independently? For example, it might be your closest buddy at times, full of positive thoughts and new ideas, and at other times, it can be a bit of a drama queen. Perhaps you've experienced butterflies in your stomach when speaking to a stranger or felt your heart beat before a significant test. Or maybe you've had that depressing feeling when you believe you've made a mistake and find it difficult to move past it. You're not by yourself! Everybody's ideas and emotions go through ups and downs.

Imagine your brain as a supercomputer. It is extremely intelligent and capable of doing incredible things, such as helping you recall the lyrics to your favorite songs, solve puzzles, and learn new skills. However, it occasionally runs unhelpful programs, just like a computer.

Consider that while you're playing a game, your brain occasionally unintentionally presses the "worry,""frustration," or even "sad" buttons. These buttons can elicit a wide range of emotions and make overcoming daily obstacles difficult.

Imagine that you are attempting to join the school's soccer squad. Even though you've put in a lot of practice, you begin to worry about whether you'll be good enough as the tryouts approach. What if I get laughed at by everyone? You feel anxious and even a little queasy when you think about these things. You may begin to think, "What's the point?" and stop practicing. I'm simply going to make a mistake." Can you see how that operates? A single negative thought ("I'm not good enough") triggers a negative emotion (anxiety), which in turn triggers a negative behavior (avoidance of practice). It resembles a domino effect!

The goal of this workbook is to provide you with the skills necessary to become a "brain trainer." When the "worry" or "frustration" buttons are pressed, you'll learn how to take control of your thoughts and emotions.

Cognitive behavioral therapy, or CBT for short, is what we'll be looking at. Don't be alarmed by the fancy name! Simply put, cognitive behavioral therapy (CBT) teaches you to be more conscious of your ideas and how they influence your emotions and behavior. Unlocking your brain's superpowers and putting them to good use is like learning a secret code!

These pages contain entertaining exercises, real-world examples, and practical advice to assist you:

- **Challenge negative thinking:** Learn how to transform those "wobbly" notions into more sensible and beneficial ones.
- **Understand your thoughts and feelings**: Acknowledge what's happening within your head and body.

- **Manage challenging emotions:** Create coping mechanisms for difficult emotions such as sadness, rage, and anxiety.
- **Build resilience and confidence:** Acquire the ability to overcome obstacles and have faith in oneself.

Prepare to take control of your thoughts and build a better, more contented version of yourself! Let's begin

# CHAPTER ONE

# UNDERSTANDING CBT AND THE THOUGHT-FEELING-ACTION CONNECTION

---

*"The greatest weapon against stress is our ability to choose one thought over another."* – William James

Have you ever wondered why it may be so difficult to get out of bed on some days while on others you feel like you can conquer the world? Much of it is related to your ideas and what's happening inside your head. Imagine your mind as a bustling metropolis that is always humming with activity. Like automobiles, some thoughts are speeding along, others are moving slowly, some are obeying the law, and some—well, let's just say they might be taking some diversions.

Discovering how this incredible metropolis functions inside your thoughts is the main goal of this chapter. We'll explore what cognitive behavioral therapy (CBT) is and why it's like having a mental superpower.

**Let's begin with a tale.** Consider Alex and Maya, two pals, preparing for a significant school presentation. Normally rather self-assured, Alex has been experiencing some anxiety lately. "What if I mess up?" Alex ponders. "What if everyone laughs at me?" Alex begins to avoid training because these thoughts make their stomach feel constricted. Even the night before the presentation, they struggle to fall asleep.

However, Maya also has pre-presentation anxiety. However, she makes an effort to adopt a different perspective when those "what if" scenarios occur. "All right," she thinks, "I might make a mistake, but everyone does. I know that I'm ready because I've practiced a lot." Maya concentrates on the things she "can" manage, such as honing her presentation skills, arranging her notes and delivering them. Although she still experiences some anxiety, she is able to control it and deliver an excellent presentation.

In what ways does Alex vary from Maya? It's not as though Maya doesn't think bad things. Everyone does! The distinction is in the way they "react" to such ideas. Alex becomes engrossed in the "what ifs," allowing them to dictate their emotions and behavior. Although Maya is aware of the concerns, she resists letting them control her. She thinks differently in order to control her anxieties.

Learning to become conscious of your ideas and how they impact your emotions and behavior is the main goal of cognitive behavioral therapy. It's about learning how to become your own "thought detective" and confronting harmful thought patterns.

What precisely "is" CBT, then? Cognitive behavioral therapy is what it stands for. Your thoughts are referred to as cognitive, and your acts as behavioral. The foundation of cognitive behavioral therapy is the notion that our ideas, feelings, and behaviors are interconnected.

Consider it similar to a three-legged stool. The entire stool is unstable if one leg is unsteady. Unpleasant ideas can result in unpleasant emotions, which can subsequently result in negative behavior. Take a moment to return to Alex. They experienced worry and avoidance (not practicing, difficulty sleeping) as a result of their pessimistic ideas ("What if I mess up?"). They avoided the scenario as a result of these feelings. This is a famous illustration of the relationship between cognition, emotion, and action.

Think about playing a video game now. You are playing a difficult level, and you continue to lose. "I'm awful at this game," you may begin to think. This level is unbeatable. You may feel demoralized and frustrated by these ideas. You may even want to give up playing completely. But what if you had a different perspective? What if you told yourself, "I can figure this it out, even though this level is a challenge? I'll attempt an alternative tactic." You can feel more motivated and positive when you think like this. You're more likely to persevere and find success in the end.

See how everything is influenced by your thoughts? They may have an impact on your actions, feelings, and even how you see the outside world. It is crucial to comprehend this connection because of this. It's the initial step towards mastering your thoughts and building a happier, more satisfying existence.

**Try this enjoyable activity**: Consider a moment when you were truly joyful. At that moment, what was on your mind? Now consider a moment when you experienced sadness or anger. What were you thinking about at the time? Is it evident to you how your thoughts affected your emotions?

As an additional illustration, suppose a friend abruptly cancels arrangements. "They don't care about me," you could think. They most likely no longer want to spend time with me. Feelings of rejection and hurt can result from these beliefs. However, what if you took a different approach? Imagine thinking, "Perhaps something came up for them. Later, I'll question them about it. You can prevent rash decisions and needless agitation by adopting this method of thinking.

The main goal of cognitive behavioral therapy (CBT) is to increase your awareness of your ideas, particularly the automatic ones that enter your mind without your conscious awareness. These habitual ideas can significantly affect your feelings and behavior, and they are frequently negative or ineffective.

In the upcoming chapter, we will go deeper into these kinds of ideas. Just keep in mind that your thoughts have tremendous power for the time being. They function similarly to the control panel for your feelings and behavior. You may take control and start living a happier, more satisfying life by learning how they operate. It's like discovering a new superpower: the ability to think positively!

## WHAT ARE CBT AND WHY DOES IT

## MATTER?

*"You are the bows from which your children as living arrows are sent forth."* – Khalil Gibran (While not directly about CBT, this quote highlights the powerful influence we have, and CBT can help us use that influence positively.)

Envision learning how to ride a bicycle. It is shaky and frightening at first. You may become frustrated, scrape your knees, and fall a few times. "I'm never going to get this," you may even think. I simply can't ride a bike well." You may become disheartened by these ideas and consider giving up. However, what if someone gave you an alternative perspective? What if they declared that falling is acceptable? When learning, everyone does. Keeping trying is what matters. You get stronger and more self-assured every time you get back on the bike.

Encouragement like this can have a profound impact. It can assist you in conquering your fear and continuing to practice till you finally master riding your bike.

Cognitive behavioral therapy (CBT) helps you understand your thoughts and feelings and create methods for overcoming obstacles. It's like having that supportive voice inside your brain.

It's not about denying painful emotions or acting as though everything is fine. It's more about understanding what's happening within your head and gaining the skills necessary to properly control your thoughts and emotions.

Imagine your mind as a garden. Weeds are those unhelpful or negative ideas that can make you feel bad sometimes. CBT is similar to learning how to spot weeds and rip them out, replacing them with constructive and uplifting ideas that resemble lovely flowers. It all comes down to developing a positive outlook that will allow you to develop and flourish.

Imagine that you are about to take a significant test. You may begin to worry, "What if I don't succeed? What if my intelligence is inadequate? You may experience tension and anxiety as a result of these ideas. You may become sleep deprived, lose your appetite, or even begin to shun studying completely. This is a well-known illustration of how negative ideas may influence your emotions and behavior.

However, you can learn to confront such negative beliefs with cognitive behavioral therapy. You could wonder, "Is there any concrete proof that I'm going to fail? Have I failed every other test that I took? What can I do to boost my confidence and get ready for the test? **You might begin to realize that your anxieties may not be grounded in reality by posing these questions.**

**Realistic and constructive thoughts, such as** "I've studied hard, and I'm going to do my best," can begin to replace those pessimistic ones. I'll gain knowledge from the experience even if I don't receive a perfect grade.

CBT isn't limited to treating major issues like depression or exam anxiety. It can also assist with common problems, such as overcoming shyness when meeting new people, controlling anger when someone cuts in line, or handling frustration when you lose a game. It's a collection of abilities that you can employ to deal with a variety of circumstances throughout your life.

**Here's a more illustration:** Imagine seeing a gathering of unfamiliar children at a party. You may be reluctant to approach them because you are bashful. "What if they don't like me?" you may ask yourself. What if people believe I'm strange? You can find yourself alone during the entire party as a result of these uneasy thoughts.

CBT, however, teaches you to question those ideas. You might tell yourself that most people are amiable and accepting, and that everyone experiences shyness occasionally. "I'm going to try to introduce myself, but it is okay to feel a little nervous," you can tell yourself. The worst case scenario is that they might not want to speak with me, but that's acceptable. I can always speak with another person. You may alter your feelings and behavior by altering the way you think. It's possible that you'll meet new people!

The fact that CBT is beyond talking about your issues is one of its fascinating features. The goal is to acquire useful abilities that you may apply to your daily life. It's similar to picking up a new sport. You don't merely sit around discussing basketball skills. You practice shooting, passing, and dribbling on the court.

CBT works similarly. You pick up skills for controlling your emotions, confronting bad thoughts, and altering your behavior. Additionally, you get better at applying these talents the more you exercise them.

Try this enjoyable activity: Consider a moment when you were extremely irritated. At that moment, what was on your mind? What did you do? Imagine for a moment that you had acquired some CBT abilities. What other course of action could you have taken? What other ideas might have crossed your mind? What other steps might you have taken?

CBT is similar to having a toolbox full of mental health tools. These resources can assist you:

1.  Identify Negative Thoughts: Acquire the ability to identify the harmful thoughts that enter your mind.

2. Challenge negative thoughts: Learn how to question negative thoughts and determine whether they are true.

3. Reframe negative thoughts: Learn how to transform negative thoughts into more balanced and positive ones.

4. Manage emotions: Create coping mechanisms for challenging emotions such as sadness, anger, and anxiety.

5. Change behaviors: Learn how to break bad habits and form better ones.

CBT is empowering. It equips you with the means to take charge of your feelings, ideas, and behavior. It's about developing into your own "thought coach," assisting yourself in overcoming obstacles and leading a more contented, healthy existence. It's not about altering your identity. Learning to become the best version of yourself is the goal.

## UNDERSTANDING THE THOUGHT-FEELING-ACTION CONNECTION

*"Watch your thoughts, they become words. Watch your words, they become actions. Watch your actions, they*

*become habits. Watch your habits, they become character. Watch your character, it becomes your destiny."* – Frank Outlaw (This quote beautifully illustrates the interconnectedness of thoughts, words, actions, and ultimately, our lives, which is central to the core of CBT.)

Have you ever observed how your mood may be drastically altered by a single thought? Imagine yourself singing your favorite song as you stroll down the street, feeling rather content. All of a sudden, you realize that you haven't done something—a homework assignment, a commitment you made, or perhaps just that you forgot to pack lunch. "Oh no, I forgot!" is the one thought that may change your mood in an instant. Your shoulders may sag, your smile may vanish, and you may even experience a slight knot in your stomach.

This is the relationship between thought and emotion in action. The power of our thoughts is tremendous. These words don't merely float around in our minds; they actually affect our emotions. Furthermore, our actions are influenced by our emotions. The basis of cognitive behavioral therapy is this whole thought-feeling-action link.

Let's take it one step farther. Let's say you are thrilled to attend a friend's birthday celebration. The games you'll play, the cake you'll eat, and the pleasures you'll have are all on your mind. Happiness, enthusiasm, and anticipation are the positive emotions that result from these optimistic beliefs. These good emotions then affect your behavior, such as making plans for what to dress, coming up with a present, or even phoning your friend to see who else is going.

Let's now consider an alternative situation. You're anxious about an upcoming test. "What if I fail?" is what's on your mind. What if my intelligence is inadequate? Anxiety, worry, and self-doubt are bad emotions brought on by these negative beliefs.

These unpleasant emotions may subsequently affect your behavior, causing you to avoid studying, have difficulty falling asleep, or even feel nauseous. See how it functions? It resembles a domino effect. The process begins with a thought, progresses to a sensation, and ultimately impacts an action. And depending on the original idea's character, this chain reaction may or may not be beneficial.

Here's an example from actual life: David and Sarah, two students, both receive poor quiz scores. Sarah's initial reaction is, "I'm so dumb. I will never be proficient in this subject. Feelings of discouragement and pessimism result from this thought. Then, wondering, "What's the point?" she might decide not to study for the upcoming test. In any case, I'm going to fail." In contrast, David's response is different. "Okay, I didn't do well on this quiz, but I can learn from my mistakes," is his initial idea. I'll speak with the instructor to find out how I can do better. Feelings of resolve and motivation result from this idea. He might then begin to put more effort into his studies, seek the teacher's assistance, and perhaps create a study group with his classmates.

David and Sarah experienced the same thing: receiving a poor quiz score. However, they had rather distinct "feelings" and "actions" as a result of their divergent "thoughts" about the circumstances. David's more constructive and optimistic thoughts produced useful acts and happy feelings, whereas Sarah's negative thoughts produced negative feelings and harmful behaviors.

This is why it's so crucial to comprehend the relationship between cognition, feeling, and action. You can alter the chain reaction with its help. You can alter your emotions and behavior if you can learn to recognize and confront unfavorable beliefs.

Try this enjoyable activity: Consider a recent event that caused you to feel anxious or angry. Put the following in writing: What transpired?

- Your thoughts: What were you thinking about at the time?

- Your emotions: What emotions did you experience?

Your behavior: How did you behave? Examine what you typed down now. Do you see how your ideas, feelings, and actions are related to each other? Did your sensations stem from your thoughts? Did your emotions affect what you did?

As an additional illustration, consider yourself trying out for the school play. You may be thinking, "What if I don't remember my lines? What if I appear foolish on stage?

Anxiety and trepidation may result from these thoughts. Then, you can opt not to practice at all.

However, you can alter your feelings and behavior if you can alter the way you think. "It's acceptable to feel a little anxious," you may tell yourself. Everyone does. I've rehearsed my lines, and I'll try my hardest. It will be enjoyable even if I don't land the lead part. Feelings of enthusiasm and confidence can result from these more optimistic thinking. After that, you might enthusiastically rehearse your lines and perform well at the audition.

A useful technique for comprehending both yourself and other people is the thought-feeling-action relationship. It enables us to understand why we respond in particular ways to various circumstances.

Additionally, it provides us with the means to transform our lives for the better. We may begin to take charge of our emotions and behaviors and build a more contented, joyful, and healthy existence by developing a greater awareness of our thoughts. It's similar to having mental superpowers!

## SELF-REFLECTION QUESTIONS

1. Think about a recent situation where you felt a strong emotion (like anger, sadness, or anxiety). What were the thoughts that were going through your head at that time?

_____

_____

_____

2. Can you identify a recurring negative thought pattern in your life? What situations trigger this thought?

_____

_____

_____

3. How do your thoughts influence your actions? Can you think of a specific example where a thought led to a particular behavior?

_____

_____

_____

4. Are there any thoughts you tend to believe without questioning them? Are these thoughts helpful or unhelpful?

_____

_____

_____

5. What is one small step you can take today to become more aware of your thoughts and how they affect you?

_____

_____

_____

## TRANSFORMATIVE EXERCISES

1. Thought Record: Create a simple chart with four columns: Situation, Thought, Feeling, and Action. Whenever you experience a strong emotion, fill out the chart. This will help you see the connection between your thoughts, feelings, and actions.

2. Thought Challenge: When you notice a negative thought, ask yourself: "Is this thought really true? Is there any evidence to support it? Is there another way to look at this situation?"

3. Positive Affirmations: Create a list of positive statements about yourself (e.g., "I am capable,""I am strong,""I am learning and growing"). Read these affirmations aloud to yourself every day.

4. Mindful Breathing: When you start to feel overwhelmed by negative thoughts or emotions, take a few deep breaths. Focus on your breath and try to clear your mind. This can help you calm down and regain control.

5. "Act as if": Even if you're feeling nervous or unsure, try "acting as if" you're confident and

capable. Sometimes, simply changing your behavior can actually change how you feel. For example, if you're nervous about public speaking, practices "acting as if" you are a confident speaker.

# CHAPTER TWO

# MEET YOUR THOUGHTS: THE

# GOOD, THE BAD, AND

# THE WOBBLY

---

*"The mind is everything. What you think you become."* –
Buddha

Ever wonder why some days you feel like you're on top of the world, ready to conquer anything, while other days you just want to curl up in a ball and hide? A lot of it has to do with your thoughts. Think of your mind like a busy city. There are lots of different vehicles – thoughts – zooming around. Some are like speedy race cars, full of energy and excitement. Others are like slow-moving trucks, carrying worries and doubts. And then there are the wobbly bicycles, those unsure thoughts that make you feel a little off-balance.

This chapter is all about getting to know your thoughts – the good, the bad, and the wobbly – and how they affect how you feel and act.

First, let's do a little thought exercise. Consider that you are about to present in class. What ideas could be racing through your head? Perhaps, you were thinking something along the lines of "I'm going to mess this up," or "Everyone will laugh at me." Negative ideas like those might make you feel a lot of different emotions, including fear, anxiety, and nervousness.

Try thinking something different now: "I've practiced this, and I'm prepared," or "Even if I make a mistake, it's okay." These are more upbeat ideas that might increase your self-esteem and calm you down considerably.

The intriguing thing is that the actual presentation hasn't even taken place yet. The only thing influencing your feelings is your "thoughts" regarding the presentation. This is the secret to realizing the power of our thoughts. These aren't just words that are circling about in our minds. They directly affect our feelings and even how we behave.

Consider a moment when you were ecstatic about something, such as attending a party or taking a vacation. It is likely that you were thinking a lot of good things, such as "This is going to be so much fun!" You must have felt energetic and delighted after thinking those things. Additionally, that enthusiasm may have caused you to behave differently; perhaps you were more gregarious, talkative, or you even helped with the preparations.

On the other hand, recall a period of time when you were depressed or anxious. Maybe you didn't perform well on an exam or you got into an argument with a friend. You were likely thinking negative thoughts like "I'm a failure" or "My friend is mad at me." Those were likely depressing, irate, or disappointing thoughts. You may have withdrawn from your friends, avoided doing your homework, or even yelled at someone as a result of those emotions.

**This is how it looks**:

- Positive thought: "I'm good at this!"  ⟶
  Emotion: Positivity  ⟶ Action: Makes a lot of effort, succeeds.

- Negative thought:"I'm going to fail."  ⟶
  Emotion: Apprehensive ⟶  Action: Gives up, avoids attempting

See how it functions? In your mind, your thoughts are like tiny seeds sown. Good thoughts develop into emotions of joy, self-assurance, and inspiration. Depressing ideas develop into emotions like fear, rage, and despair. Additionally, you can learn to choose which thoughts to nurture, much like a gardener tends to their plants.

Now, let us discuss many types of thinking. Although we have already discussed positive and negative ideas, there are additional types as well.

There exist pragmatic ideas that are grounded in data and facts. For instance, if you put a lot of effort into studying for an exam, a reasonable response might be, "I'm well-prepared for this test." Next are irrational ideas that are frequently overstated and not grounded on reality. An unrealistic idea could be, for instance, "I'm a complete idiot" if you answer one test question incorrectly.

The **"all-or-nothing"** mentality is another kind of thought. At this point, everything appears completely black and white, with no gray areas in between. For instance, "If I'm not the best at something, I'm a total failure." Because it ignores errors and flaws, which are inevitable in life, this way of thinking can be extremely damaging.

There are also **"wobbly"** thoughts, which aren't really pleasant or negative but leave you feeling uncertain and perplexed. For instance, "I think I did okay on the project, but I'm not sure." These erratic ideas can be problematic since, if you're not watchful, they might occasionally result in pessimistic thinking.

Let us examine several instances from the real world. Consider Alex, a young person attempting to join the school's soccer squad. "I'm a pretty good player," said Alex, and "I'm excited to try out." However, Alex worries about things like "what if I don't make the team?" and "what if everyone's better than me?" Additionally, there are the shaky notions, such as "I think I'm good enough, but I'm not really sure."

Here's another illustration. Consider Sarah, a teenager, who receives an invitation to a party. For example, Sarah thinks positively, "It will be fun to hang out with my friends.""What if I don't know anyone there?" is one of her pessimistic ideas. Together with "What if no one talks to me?" This is followed by shaky ideas such as "I hope I have a good time."

What possible effects might Sarah's thoughts have on her emotions and behavior? She is likely to feel thrilled and anticipate the celebration if she concentrates on the good thoughts. However, she may become nervous and maybe decide not to go if she keeps thinking about the bad things. Additionally, she may feel uncertain and apprehensive if she keeps thinking erratic thoughts.

You now have the opportunity to consider your own ideas. Consider a recent experience that may have made you feel pleased, sad, furious, or afraid. What were the things that were on your mind at that moment? Were they unsteady, negative, or positive? How did you feel about those thoughts? And how did those emotions influence what you did?

Try this entertaining activity. Using a sheet of paper, sketch three columns. The columns should be labeled "Positive Thoughts," "Negative Thoughts," and "Wobbly Thoughts." In the relevant column, list every idea that comes to mind while considering a particular scenario. You can become more conscious of your thoughts by doing this.

Consider visualizing your ideas as clouds floating in the sky as an additional exercise. Some stormy, gloomy clouds stand for pessimistic ideas. Positive ideas are symbolized by other clouds that are sunny and brilliant. Additionally, some clouds have a wispy, gray appearance, which symbolizes shaky ideas. Observe the passing clouds and note which ones you find yourself concentrating on.

You can learn from this that you don't have to get sucked into every thought that crosses your mind. Which clouds you want to focus on and which you want to ignore are up to you.

The first step in controlling your emotions and developing resilience is becoming conscious of your thoughts. Similar to how a detective looks into a case, you can look into your own thoughts and discover which ones are useful and which are not. We'll discover some awesome strategies for combating those pessimistic ideas and transforming them into emotional wellbeing superheroes in the upcoming chapter.

# RECOGNIZING YOUR THOUGHTS:

# TUNING INTO YOUR INNER VOICE

*"The greatest discovery of my generation is that a human being can alter his life by altering his attitudes."*
– William James

Have you ever seen how your entire mood can abruptly shift after a seemingly insignificant event, such as someone bumping into you in the corridor or your favorite food running out? You go from being joyful to being grumpy in a matter of seconds, as if a switch were to flip. What is happening there? Often, how you "interpret" an experience—that is, the ideas that come to mind—rather than the event itself is what alters your mood.

This subchapter focuses on developing the skills necessary to identify your ideas, become a thought detective, and comprehend how your thoughts affect your emotions and behavior. Imagine it as a way to connect with your inner voice. Our minds are like a radio station that never stops playing—we all have a steady stream of ideas.

The music is loud and startling at moments, quiet and mellow at others, and cheerful and uplifting at others. Understanding what your inner voice is saying to you and learning to listen to it are crucial.

First, let's look at an example. Consider yourself feeling a little overburdened by a school assignment that is due tomorrow. What types of ideas could be running through your mind? Perhaps you are thinking something along the lines of "This is too difficult, I'm going to fail," or "I'll never be able to finish this on time." Negative ideas like those can cause you to feel uncomfortable, stressed, and even demoralized.

Alternate set of thoughts would be "I can break this project down into smaller steps," or "I've done difficult projects before, and I can do this too." These are more constructive and upbeat thoughts that might boost your self-esteem and drive.

The intriguing aspect is that the project has remained unchanged. Your feelings regarding the project are solely a result of your "thoughts" about it. Cognitive behavioral therapy (CBT) is based on the fundamental tenet that our thoughts, feelings, and behaviors are interconnected. We can begin to comprehend how our thoughts affect our feelings and behavior by learning to identify them.

Think about a moment when you achieved something for which you were truly proud, such as scoring a goal in a soccer match or receiving a high test score. Most likely, you were thinking a lot of positive things, such as "I'm smart and capable!" or "I'm a great player!" I'm sure those sentiments gave you a sense of confidence and happiness. Additionally, you might have behaved differently as a result of that confidence; perhaps you were more open to trying new things or accepting challenges.

Conversely, consider a period of time when you were depressed or disheartened. Perhaps you didn't receive an invitation to a party or you got into a fight with a friend. It's likely that you were thinking negative ideas like "Nobody wants to be around me" or "My friend doesn't like me anymore." You most likely felt depressed, alone, or rejected when you believed those things. And your behavior may have been influenced by those emotions; you may have distanced yourself from your friends, refused to attend school, or even lost your temper with a member of your family.

It resembles a domino effect (chain reaction):

- Positive thought "I can do this!" ➡Emotion: Self-assured ➡Action: Makes a concerted effort and succeeds.
- Negative thought "I'm going to mess up." ➡Emotion: Nervous ➡Action: Does not attempt, makes mistakes

See how it functions? In your mind, your thoughts are like tiny seeds that you sown. Good thoughts develop into emotions of joy, self-assurance, and inspiration. Depressing ideas develop into emotions like fear, rage, and despair. Additionally, you can learn to choose which thoughts to nurture, much like a gardener tends to their plants.

Let's now discuss the many kinds of thinking. Positive and negative ideas have already been discussed, but there are other types as well. There are reasonable ideas that are supported by data and facts.

If you were rehearsing your lines for a play, for instance, a realistic idea may be, "I'm well-prepared for this audition." Then there are unrealistic ideas, which are frequently overblown and not grounded in reality. When you forget a line during the audition, for instance, you can think unrealistically, "I'm a terrible actor, and I'll never get a part in a play."

The "all-or-nothing" mentality is another kind of thought. At this point, everything appears completely black and white, with no gray areas in between. For instance, "I'm a total loser if I don't win the race." Because it ignores errors and flaws, which are inevitable in life, this way of thinking can be extremely damaging.

Then there are the "should" thoughts, in which you persuade yourself that instead of accepting things as they are, they "should" be. For instance, "I should be able to get all my homework done in one hour." When reality doesn't live up to your expectations, these "should" thoughts can cause guilt and dissatisfaction.

Let's examine a few more instances from actual life. Consider David, a young child who is attempting to learn how to skateboard. David thinks positively, saying things like "I'm having fun learning" and "I'm getting better at balancing." "What if I fall and break my arm?" and "What if the other kids laugh at me?" are some of David's pessimistic concerns. The "should" notions follow, such as "I should be able to do this perfectly by now."

What impact do you believe David's thoughts may have on his emotions and behavior? David will likely feel motivated and confident if he concentrates on the good ideas, which will encourage him to continue practicing. However, David may become terrified and disheartened and decide to give up if he allows himself to become engrossed in the pessimistic ideas. Additionally, David may become impatient and frustrated if he concentrates on the "should" thinking, which could impede his progress.

Here's another illustration. Consider Maria, an adolescent who is anxious about asking someone to the school ball. "It would be fun to go to the dance with him," Maria thinks positively, and "He seems like a nice person." "What if he says no?" and "What if he thinks I'm weird?" are some of her negative ideas, though. And then the shaky thoughts, such as "I hope he likes me."

What possible effects might Maria's thoughts have on her emotions and behavior? She will likely feel more confident and be more inclined to ask him if she concentrates on the good ideas. However, she can become too anxious and choose not to question him at all if she keeps thinking about the bad things. Additionally, she may feel uncertain and hesitant if she is hooked on the shaky thoughts. It's your turn now to consider your own ideas.

Consider a recent event that affected you emotionally, such as happiness, sadness, anger, or fear. At that moment, what were the thoughts that were running through your mind? Were they unsteady, "should," negative, or positive? What emotions did those thoughts evoke in you? Additionally, how did those feelings affect your actions?

Try this enjoyable hobby: Divide each page of your notebook into four sections: "Should" Thoughts, Wobbly Thoughts, Negative Thoughts, and Positive Thoughts. Try to keep track of your thoughts during the day and record them in the relevant section.

This can make you more conscious of the ways in which your thoughts impact you. Try visualizing your thoughts as leaves floating down a river as an additional exercise.

You may see the passing leaves without becoming entangled in them. This can assist you in realizing that you are not required to accept every idea that enters your mind. You can just look at them without passing judgment.

The first step in controlling your emotions and developing resilience is becoming conscious of your thoughts. Similar to how a detective looks into a case, you can look into your own thoughts and discover which ones are useful and which are not. We will discover some useful strategies for confronting negative thoughts and transforming them into constructive and constructive ones in the upcoming section.

## IDENTIFY DIFFERENT TYPES OF THOUGHTS: HELPFUL VS. UNHELPFUL

*"The happiness of your life depends upon the quality of your thoughts."* – Marcus Aurelius

Have you ever had the feeling that your thoughts are flying around in your head like leaves in a storm? You feel fantastic when you think some of those thoughts— excited, self-assured, and prepared to take on the world. Not so much for others. They could make you feel depressed, anxious, or even irate. Learning to recognize the various types of thoughts that pass through your mind and knowing which ones offer sunshine and which ones bring storms is like receiving a weather report for your mind. We'll discuss the distinction between constructive and destructive ideas and how identifying them can help you better regulate your emotions and behavior.

Let us begin with a situation that is relatable. Consider learning a new skill, such as riding a skateboard or playing an instrument. You will inevitably make blunders because you are still a novice. What kinds of ideas could cross your mind?

**Disadvantageous Thoughts**:

- "This is really bad of me. I'll never get it.
- "I am inferior to everyone else. I feel very ashamed.
- "I keep making mistakes. I ought to give up."
- "This is too difficult. I'm not intelligent enough.

Helpful thoughts

- "Mistakes are OK. In this way, I learn.
- "Everyone begins in some capacity. With practice, I'll improve."
- "I'm making progress, even if it's small."
- "I can ask for help if I need it."

Are you able to distinguish between these two different ways of thinking? The negative ideas depress you, irritate you, and may even make you want to give up. They resemble tiny obstacles in your educational journey.

Conversely, the constructive ideas are upbeat and encouraging. They encourage you to persevere through difficult times. They serve as mental cheerleaders, encouraging you to keep going.

Consider a moment when you were gaining knowledge. What were some of the ideas that crossed your mind? Were they primarily beneficial or detrimental? What impact did those thoughts have on your emotions and behavior? They inspired you to continue, or did they make you want to quit?

In actuality, everyone has both beneficial and detrimental thoughts. It's quite typical. Knowing how to identify them and comprehend their effects is crucial. Though they may seem plausible, unhelpful ideas aren't necessarily grounded in reality. They may be overly dramatic, pessimistic, and even little cruel. They may claim that you're not good enough, that no one likes you, or that you're a failure. However, those are only opinions, not facts. You have the ability to confront those negative ideas and decide to concentrate on more constructive ones.

Let's examine some prevalent categories of harmful thinking in more detail:

- **Thinking in terms of all or nothing**: At this point, everything appears as black and white, devoid of any gray areas. For instance, "I'm a failure if I don't receive straight as." Errors and faults are inevitable in life, but this way of thinking ignores them.

- **The act of catastrophizing**: This is the point at which you anticipate the worst, even in the absence of supporting data. For instance, "My life is over if I don't make the team." This may cause needless concern and stress.

- **Oversimplifying**: This occurs when you extrapolate a single unfavorable experience to every circumstance. For instance, "I messed up on this one test, so I'm bad at all subjects." This can make you feel discouraged and less likely to try.

- **Personalizing**: This is the act of placing the responsibility for circumstances beyond your control on oneself. For instance, "My friend is in a bad mood, it must be because of something I did." Guilt and self-blame may result from this.

- **Psychological Reading**: This is the situation where you presume to know what other people are thinking without genuinely questioning them. For instance, "She must be upset with me because she didn't say hello." Misunderstandings and wounded sentiments may result from this.

**Let's now examine some real-world instances of these detrimental thought patterns**.

Consider a little child named Leo who is attempting to audition for the school play. He has an all-or-nothing mentality: "I'm a total failure if I don't get the lead role." The statement, "If I mess up my lines, everyone will laugh at me, and I'll never be able to show my face again," is another example of his catastrophizing behavior. "The drama teacher looked at me funny; she probably thinks I'm a terrible actor," he says, reading his mind.

What impact do you believe Leo's thoughts may have on his emotions and behavior? He is likely to have extreme anxiety and nervousness, which may make it even more difficult for him to perform well during the audition. Because he is so terrified of failure, he may even choose not to try out at all.

**Here's another illustration**. Consider a teenage girl named Maya and her friend arguing. Maya is making it personal when she says, "My friend is being mean to me; it must be because I did something wrong." Additionally, she is generalizing when she says, "I always ruin my friendships. Simply put, I struggle to make friends.

What possible effects might Maya's thoughts have on her emotions and behavior? It's likely that she may experience hurt and distress, and she may even begin to avoid her friend. Additionally, she might begin to think that she is not good at making friends, which could make it more difficult for her to establish new friends later on.

It's your turn now to consider your own ideas. Try to think of a recent event that caused you to feel anxious, stressed, or unhappy. At that moment, what were the thoughts that were running through your mind? Were they beneficial or detrimental? Can you name any of the harmful thought patterns we discussed, such as mind reading, catastrophizing, and all-or-nothing thinking?

Try this enjoyable hobby: Take a piece of paper and mark the center with a line. On each side, put "Helpful Thoughts," and "Unhelpful Thoughts." List the ideas that spring to mind in the relevant column after considering a certain scenario. This can make you more conscious of the ways in which you think and how they affect you.

You might also try visualizing your thoughts as various characters in a play. Some characters, such as the sage old owl who offers sound counsel, are useful and encouraging. Other characters, such as the sulky troll who only perceives the negative aspects of things, are unhelpful and negative. See which characters tend to take center stage and try to determine which ones reflect you're various ideas. This can assist you in realizing that you have the ability to choose which characters you choose to hear.

One of the most important steps in developing emotional wellbeing and resilience is learning to distinguish between constructive and destructive ideas. It's similar to learning to distinguish between junk food and healthful food. In order to feel strong and capable, you want to feed your mind with constructive and upbeat ideas. We'll learn how to confront those negative beliefs and swap them out for more realistic and upbeat ones in the upcoming section.

## SELF-REFLECTION QUESTIONS

1. Think about a time you felt really happy. What were some of the thoughts you were having at the time? How did those thoughts make you feel?

   _____

   _____

   _____

2. Now think about a time you felt really upset or worried. What were some of the thoughts you were having then? How did those thoughts make you feel?

   _____

   _____

   _____

3. Can you think of a time when your thoughts didn't match reality? For example, did you ever think something bad was going to happen, and then it didn't?

   _____

   _____

   _____

4. What are some of the most common thoughts that go through your head? Are they mostly positive, negative, or a mix of both?

_____

_____

_____

5. Do you notice any patterns in your thinking? For example, do you tend to worry a lot about what other people think?

_____

_____

_____

## TRANSFORMATIVE EXERCISES

1. Thought Diary: Get a notebook and divide each page into three columns: Situation, Thought, and Feeling. Throughout the day, try to notice when your mood changes. Write down the situation, the thought that popped into your head, and the feeling you experienced. This will help you see the connection between your thoughts and feelings.

2. Thought Bubbles: Draw a cartoon version of you. When you notice a thought, imagine it inside a thought bubble above your head. Try to identify if the thought is helpful or unhelpful. If it's

unhelpful, imagine popping the bubble and letting the thought go.

3. Thought Challenge: When you notice an unhelpful thought, ask yourself: Is this thought really true? What's the evidence for and against it? Is there another way to look at the situation? Try to reframe the thought into something more balanced and realistic.

4. Positive Affirmations: Come up with a few positive statements about you, like "I am capable,""I am strong," or "I am loved." Repeat these affirmations to yourself regularly, especially when you're feeling down. This can help to boost your self-esteem and create more positive thought patterns.

5. Mindful Breathing: When you're feeling overwhelmed by your thoughts, take a few deep breaths. Focus on the sensation of the air going in and out of your body. This can help to calm your mind and give you a break from your thoughts. You can even imagine your worries as clouds passing by in the sky as you breathe.

# CHAPTER THREE

# DECODING YOUR FEELINGS:

# FROM HAPPY TO FRUSTRATED

# AND EVERYTHING IN BETWEEN

---

*"Feelings are just visitors, let them come and go."* –
Mooji

Have you ever observed all the various hues in a rainbow? Each color—red, orange, yellow, green, blue, indigo, and violet—is distinct and lovely in its own right. We experience a range of emotions that color our life, much like a rainbow. Like a brilliant yellow sunbeam, we can experience joy and excitement at times. Sometimes, like a dark blue raincloud, we may feel depressed or lonely. Then there are moments when we experience frustration or anger, which is like a crimson lightning strike.

This chapter focuses on discovering the amazing realm of emotions, ranging from joy to frustration and all points in between, and learning to interpret what they are attempting to convey.

Consider yourself at a birthday celebration. All of your pals are present, and there is cake, gifts, and games. How would you feel, in your opinion? I'm sure they're excited and happy. You may feel like leaping up and down with delight, your heart may be a little faster, and you may be wearing a broad smile. All of these indicate excitement and happiness, which are your body's signals that you're feeling good.

Now consider an alternative situation. You put a lot of effort into studying for the test, but you didn't receive the mark you were looking for. What do you suppose your feelings would be then? You are most likely disappointed, perhaps even a little irritated or furious. Your face may feel hot, you may have a knot in your stomach, and you may want to hide by curling up in a ball. All of these are indications that you're feeling more difficult emotions, such as disappointment, frustration, and possibly even despair.

The most crucial thing to keep in mind is that every emotion is real. The concept of a "bad" feeling does not exist. Sad or furious emotions are just as significant as pleasant ones, just as a wet day is as significant as a bright one. Each of them is a component of the human condition. Consider your emotions to be messages. They are attempting to convey a crucial message about you or your circumstances. You can take better care of yourself and make better decisions if you can comprehend those messages.

**Let's discuss some typical emotions and what they could be expressing to you:**

- **Contentment**: This sensation typically indicates that you're having fun or that something positive has happened. It can boost your motivation, energy, and optimism.

- **Sadness**: This emotion frequently arises after a loss or disappointment. Sometimes it's acceptable to be depressed. You can finally move on and handle tough emotions with the aid of sadness.

- **Anger**: This emotion may surface when you feel intimidated, unfairly treated, or as though someone has crossed your limits. Anger is a strong emotion that can inspire you to take constructive action. But it's crucial to manage your anger in a way that doesn't harm you or other people.

- **Apprehension**: This emotion is a normal reaction to danger. By warning you of possible dangers, it can keep you safe. However, there are situations in which we experience fear even in the absence of actual danger, such as when we are anxious about a potential future event.

- **Feelings of jealousy**: You may experience this emotion if you're afraid of losing something or someone that holds special meaning for you. It's critical to keep in mind that jealousy frequently stems from anxieties and to express your emotions in a constructive manner. The feeling of embarrassment when you think you've done something foolish or committed a mistake, you may have this emotion.

It's critical to keep in mind that everyone makes errors. One of the most important aspects of developing resilience is learning to forgive ourselves.

Consider a moment when you experienced each of these feelings. What was going on at the moment? Describe the bodily sensations you experienced. Which ideas were running through your mind?

Try this enjoyable hobby. Utilizing a sheet of paper, sketch a "Feelings Thermometer." Put "Low Intensity" at the bottom of the thermometer and "High Intensity" at the top. Next, write distinct feelings, such as joy, sorrow, rage, fear, etc., on various thermometer sections. Try to put your feelings on the thermometer by thinking about a recent event. This can assist you in comprehending the strength of your feelings.

Another task you could attempt is making a "Feelings Chart." Make a chart where each face stands for a particular emotion. Emojis can even be added to your chart. Check in with yourself throughout the day to see how you're feeling. Next, indicate your feeling by pointing to the face on the chart that most accurately depicts it.

You may become more conscious of your emotions and how they evolve over the day as a result. It's also critical to keep in mind that everyone has a unique emotional experience. What brings joy to one individual may bring sadness to another. Feelings can be either right or wrong. Learning to identify your emotions, comprehend what they're trying to tell you, and express them in a healthy way is crucial.

Let's examine a few instances from actual life. Consider a little child named Ethan who is upset because his favorite toy was broken by his brother. His muscles may tense, his face may become flushed, and he may feel the need to hit or yell. Ethan should be able to identify when he is feeling angry and find a constructive outlet for it, such as talking to a trusted adult or exercising, like going for a run.

Here's another illustration. Consider Sarah, an adolescent who is anxious before presenting in class. Her hands may be sweating, she may experience butterflies in her stomach, and she may find it difficult to focus. It's critical that Sarah acknowledges her anxiety and employs calming strategies to control it, such as deep breathing or encouraging self-talk.

Decoding your emotions is a lifetime process. Gaining greater awareness of your feelings and how they impact you requires time and effort. However, the more you practice, the more adept you will be at self-awareness and healthy emotional regulation. We'll discover some useful strategies for overcoming difficult emotions and enhancing resilience in the upcoming chapter.

# EXPLORING THE WORLD OF EMOTIONS: WHAT ARE THEY AND WHY DO WE HAVE THEM?

*"The most beautiful thing we can experience is the mysterious. It is the source of all true art and science."* –
Albert Einstein

Have you ever considered the reasons behind our emotions? Why do we experience joy and excitement at times and sadness or anger at others? Emotions can be a confusing whirlpool of feelings and ideas that might occasionally feel too much to handle. However, we may investigate the realm of emotions and gain a deeper understanding of them, much like scientists investigate the secrets of the cosmos. Exploring the intriguing realm of emotions—what they are, why we experience them, and how important they are to our lives—is the focus of this subchapter.

Consider yourself viewing a film. A major journey is about to begin for the main character. Your heart is racing with anticipation as the music rises and the camera pans in. An emotion is that sensation of exhilaration.

It's a multifaceted experience that encompasses your body, mind, and actions. For example, you may think,

"This is going to be amazing!" Your body may respond by producing sweaty palms, a spike in energy, and an elevated heart rate. Additionally, you might sit on the edge of your seat with your eyes fixed on the screen.

Similar to internal signals, emotions notify us of our internal and external circumstances. They aid in decision-making and help us comprehend our surroundings, much like a compass.

Consider this: you would most likely be afraid if you saw a snake in the grass. You would be motivated to distance yourself from the snake out of fear. Over time, emotions have changed to aid in our survival and well-being.

But emotions aren't only about survival. They are also essential to our relationships and general health. We can interact with people, express our wants, and go through the whole range of human experience thanks to emotions. Consider a world devoid of feelings. The place would be really boring! We wouldn't be able to feel the comfort of a friend's support, the happiness of reaching a goal, or the joy of falling in love. Let's examine a few of the main causes of our emotions:

- **Survival:** Fear is an emotion that helps us stay safe and avoid danger, as we mentioned with the snake example. If we feel endangered, we may be motivated to defend ourselves by other emotions, such as wrath.

- **Communication**: Emotions enable us to express our needs and feelings to others, even in the absence of words; for example, a grin can express joy, frown sadness, and clenched fist anger.
- **Motivation**: Emotions can inspire us to act; excitement can propel us to follow our dreams, while frustration can push us to overcome obstacles.
- **Connection**: Emotions are important in our relationships; love, joy, and empathy enable us to connect with others and form strong bonds.
- **Well-being**: Feeling a range of emotions is a normal and healthy aspect of life, and it is vital to learn to comprehend and control them.
- **Trigger**: This is the circumstance or event that sets off the feeling. It could be something internal, like a memory or thought, or something external, like a loud noise.
- **Conjectures**: How we perceive the emotion is greatly influenced by our thoughts about the trigger. For instance, you might think, "That dog is going to bite me!" if you see it sprinting in your direction. This idea is likely to make you feel afraid. In contrast, if you think, "That dog looks

friendly and wants to play," you may experience excitement.

- **Physical Feelings**: Our bodies frequently experience physical experiences in tandem with emotions. These feelings can change based on the emotion. For instance, happiness may make you feel light and energized, whereas fear may make your heart race and your palms perspire.

- **Action**: Our actions can be influenced by our feelings. For instance, enjoyment may cause you to laugh and grin, whereas fear may cause you to flee from danger.

Consider a recent instance in which you felt a powerful feeling. Is it possible to pinpoint the trigger, your thoughts, the bodily sensations you went through, and your actions?

Try this enjoyable hobby: Establish a "**Feelings Diary**." Write down the various circumstances that make you feel a certain way during the day. Give a description of the feelings, emotions, bodily sensations, and actions you experienced in each scenario. You may become more conscious of your emotional habits as a result.

One more thing you could do is play "**Emotion Charades**." While others attempt to determine the mood you are portraying, take turns playing out various emotions silently. You can learn more about the various ways that emotions can be portrayed by doing this.

It's critical to keep in mind that every person has a unique emotional experience. Something that enrages one person may not irritate another at all. Feelings can be either right or wrong. Understanding how to read your own emotional cues and interpret what they're trying to tell you is crucial.

Let's examine a few instances from actual life. Consider a little child named Maya who is depressed by the move of her best friend. Her friend's movement is the trigger. She may be thinking, "I'll never have another friend like her," and "I'm going to miss her so much." She may have a heavy sensation in her chest, tears in her eyes, and a knot in her throat. She may act in a way that distances herself from her other friends and spend a lot of time alone.

Here's another illustration. Consider David, a teenager who is eager to try out for the school's basketball team. The impending tryouts are the trigger. He may be thinking, "I'm going to be the star player!" and "I'm going to make the team!" He may experience a jolt of energy, a broad smile, and butterflies in his tummy. It's possible that he practices basketball daily and imagines himself joining the team.

Gaining insight into the realm of emotions is a lifelong process. Being more conscious of your own emotional landscape and how it affects your feelings, ideas, and behavior requires time and effort. However, you will be better able to handle life's ups and downs and create solid, wholesome relationships the more you understand emotions. We'll explore several useful techniques for handling challenging emotions and developing resilience in the upcoming subchapter.

## UNDERSTANDING HOW THOUGHTS

## AND FEELINGS INTERACT

*"You are the master of your emotions, but a slave to your thoughts."* – Elizabeth Gilbert

Have you ever experienced the crazy highs and lows of an emotional rollercoaster? One moment you're having a good time with your buddies, and the next you're depressed due to an exam. There is a lot going on behind the scenes, even if it may seem like your emotions appear suddenly.

Understanding the intriguing relationship between your thoughts and feelings is the main focus of this subchapter. It's similar to discovering the key to your emotional universe, enabling you to take control of your emotional health and comprehend why you feel the way you do.

Let's begin with a straightforward example. Imagine seeing your buddies laughing together as you pass them in the school hallway. What is the first thought that comes to mind? Your feelings will be greatly influenced by that thinking.

First Possible Thought: "It's likely that they're making fun of me." How would you feel if this were your thought? You are most likely offended, ashamed, and possibly even furious. Your stomach may begin to knot, your face may begin to get hot, and you may want to stay away from your friends.

Second Possible Thought: "They must be enjoying themselves." What are they laughing about, I wonder? Your emotions would probably be quite different with this concept. You may feel inquisitive, somewhat excluded, but not necessarily angry. You might even feel inclined to go over and join them.

The key to understanding the thought-feeling connection is that, although the situation is the same—your friends are laughing—your "thoughts" about it result in entirely different "feelings". Our thoughts are like little stories we tell ourselves about the world, and those stories have a powerful impact on our emotions. It's not just what happens to us that determines how we feel, but how we "**interpret**" what happens.

Think of it this way: Your thoughts are the seeds you plant in the garden of your mind. Helpful, positive thoughts are like planting beautiful flowers; they blossom into feelings of happiness, confidence, and joy.

On the other hand, unhelpful, negative thoughts are like planting weeds; they can choke your happiness and make you feel anxious, stressed, or depressed.

**Let's take a closer look at this connection.**

- Unhelpful Thoughts: I'm going to disappoint my parents."
- Helpful Thoughts: "Okay, I didn't do as well as I hoped. I am able to grow from my errors. "I'll talk to the teacher and see how I can improve." It's only a single test. It does not imply that I am a complete failure.

Do you see how these disparate ideas could result in disparate emotions? You would likely feel depressed, disheartened, and possibly like giving up as a result of the unhelpful thoughts.

Conversely, the constructive ideas would motivate you to keep trying and gain knowledge from the experience.

**Here's an easy formula to keep in mind:**

Thought ──────▶Feeling ─────────▶ Action

Your moods impact your behavior, and your thoughts impact your emotions. Negative ideas will probably cause you to feel negative, which may subsequently cause you to act negatively. When you think, "I'm going to mess up this presentation," for instance, you may become anxious and avoid practicing, which could ultimately result in a poor performance.

The good news is that you don't have to live with your thoughts. You have the ability to confront such negative ideas and select more practical, constructive ones. Cognitive behavioral therapy (CBT) is centered on this. It's about learning to become aware of your ideas, understanding their impact on your feelings, and changing the way you think so you can feel better and act more effectively.

Let's examine a few more instances from actual life. Consider Carlos, a little child who feels excluded from a celebration because he was not invited. He may think things like "I'm always the one who gets left out" or "Nobody likes me." He would most likely feel depressed and lonely thinking these things. "Maybe they just forgot to invite me," or "I have other friends who care about me," are some ways he might be able to counter those notions and feel a little better.

Let's look at some additional real-world examples. Think about a young youngster named Carlos who feels left out of a party because he was not invited. For example, he can believe that "I'm always the one who gets left out" or "Nobody likes me." These thoughts would probably make him feel lonely and melancholy. He could say something like, "Maybe they just forgot to invite me," or "I have other friends who care about me," to help him feel a little better.

Try this enjoyable hobby. Draw a picture of a thought bubble on a piece of paper. Write down a recent thought that caused you to feel a particular way inside the thinking bubble. Next, sketch another thinking bubble and jot down an alternative idea that would make you feel better about the same circumstance.

This will show you how altering your thoughts can alter your emotions. One more thing you may do is play "Thought Detective." Make an effort to pinpoint the ideas that cross your mind in various contexts. Consider whether these thoughts are beneficial or detrimental. Are they excessive or realistic? You may become more conscious of your thought patterns as a result.

It's like having a superpower when you realize how ideas and feelings are connected. It enables you to take charge of your feelings and build a happier, more satisfying existence. We'll discover some useful techniques in the upcoming chapters for confronting those negative thoughts and replacing them with more constructive and encouraging ones.

## SELF-REFLECTION QUESTIONS

1.  Think about a time you felt a strong emotion, like excitement or anger. What triggered that feeling? What physical sensations did you notice in your body?

    _____

    _____

    _____

2. Can you describe a time when your thoughts influenced how you felt? Did changing your thoughts change your feelings?

_____

_____

_____

3. What are some of the most common emotions you experience? What situations tend to trigger those emotions?

_____

_____

_____

4. How do you usually express your feelings? Are there any healthy or unhealthy ways you've noticed yourself reacting?

_____

_____

_____

5. What are some things you do to cope with difficult emotions, like sadness or frustration? Are these strategies helpful?

_____

_____

_____

## TRANSFORMATIVE EXERCISES

1. Feelings Check-In: Throughout the day, take a few moments to check in with yourself. Ask yourself: How am I feeling right now? Try to identify the specific emotion and rate its intensity (e.g., on a scale of 1 to 10). This helps you become more aware of your emotional state.

2. Feelings Thermometer: Draw a thermometer and label different sections with different emotions (happy, sad, angry, scared, etc.). When you experience a strong emotion, mark where it falls on the thermometer. This helps you visualize the intensity of your feelings.

3. Emotion Charades: Play charades with friends or family, acting out different emotions without speaking. This helps you become more familiar with the physical expressions of various emotions.

4. "I Feel..." Statements: Practice using "I feel..." statements to express your emotions. For example, instead of saying "You made me mad!", say "I feel angry when..." This helps you

communicate your feelings in a clear and respectful way.

5. Create a "Coping Toolkit": Make a list of activities that help you manage difficult emotions. These could include things like listening to music, spending time in nature, talking to a friend, or doing something creative. When you're feeling overwhelmed, refer to your toolkit and choose an activity that will help you cope.

# CHAPTER FOUR

# SPOTTING THINKING TRAPS:

# THOSE SNEAKY THOUGHT

# DISTORTERS

---

*"The mind is a wonderful servant, but a terrible master."*
— Robin Sharma

This chapter is all about becoming a "thought detective" and learning to recognize these thinking traps, which are sneaky thought patterns that can lead to negative feelings and unhelpful behaviors. Have you ever entered a funhouse and looked at those distorted mirrors? They twist your reflection, making you look taller, shorter, wider, or just plain silly. However, sometimes our thoughts can act like those distorted mirrors; twisting reality and making us see things in a way that's not quite accurate.

Let's say you are making cookies. Despite your meticulous attention to the recipe, you inadvertently add a bit too much salt. You don't get the exact results you were hoping for with the cookies. What might be going through your mind?

Thinking traps include these kinds of ideas. They can make you feel very crummy and aren't founded on the complete truth.

Let's examine some typical thought traps in more detail:

- **Catastrophizing**: This is when you anticipate the worst, even in the absence of supporting data. It's devastating to think, "My entire day is ruined!" due to the cookies. It's probably not true that your entire day is wrecked just because of one tiny incident.
- **Psychological Reading**: This is the situation where you presume to know what other people are

thinking without genuinely questioning them. Its mind reading to believe that "everyone is going to think I'm a failure" You don't actually know what everyone else is thinking.

- **Thinking in terms of all or nothing**: At this point, everything appears as black and white, devoid of any gray areas. Thinking "I should just give up on baking altogether" is all-or-nothing thinking. It doesn't allow for the possibility of learning from your mistakes

- **Personalization**: This is the act of placing the blame for circumstances beyond your control on yourself. Personalization would be if you were to say, "It must be because of something I did," in response to your friend getting upset. You don't know for sure why your friend is in a bad mood.

- **Should Statements**: Included in these notions are the terms "should" and "must." For instance, "I should be able to bake perfect cookies every time." These kinds of ideas might lead to needless stress and guilt.

- **Mental Filter**: This is when you only pay attention to the negative aspects of a situation and ignores the positive ones. For instance, if you receive a good grade on an exam but miss one question, and you only concentrate on the missed question that is mental filtering.

Let's look at some more real-life examples of how thinking traps can affect kids and teens. For instance, consider Alex, a student who is anxious about giving a presentation in class. He may think, "Everyone is going to laugh at me" (Mind Reading) and "I'm going to freeze up and forget everything I'm supposed to say" (Catastrophizing). These thinking traps could make him feel even more anxious and possibly cause him to stop practicing altogether.

Here's another example: Consider a depressed teen named Sarah who is feeling down because she was not invited to a party. She may think things like "I'm always the one who gets left out" (Personalization) and "Nobody likes me" (Overgeneralization), which could make her feel even more alone and cause her to distance herself from her friends.

Try this entertaining exercise: Get a piece of paper and draw a picture of a magnifying glass. Use the magnifying glass to "examine" your thoughts: Is this thought true? Is there evidence to support it? Am I falling into any thinking traps?

In the next chapter, we'll learn how to reframe those negative thoughts and turn them into positive power boosts for your emotional wellbeing. Another activity you can try is "Thought Bingo." Make bingo cards with various thinking traps (such as overgeneralization, catastrophizing, etc.) written on them.

Throughout the day, try to identify these thinking traps in your own thoughts and mark them on your bingo card. Learning to recognize thinking traps is like learning a secret code to your mind; it gives you the ability to challenge those distorted thoughts and replace them with more practical and beneficial ones.

## ALL-OR-NOTHING THINKING: SEEING

## IN BLACK AND WHITE

*"The world is not black and white; it is painted in shades of gray."* – Unknown

Did you ever notice the zebra's eye-catching black and white stripes? They are really different from one another. What if you believed that there was no middle ground and that everything in life was black and white? All-or-nothing thinking is like that. It's a mental trap in which you only consider the positive and the negative, leaving no space for anything in between. Learning to view the world in its full color and shedding light on this widespread thought trap are the main goals of this subchapter.

Consider a moment when you were learning a new skill, such as how to ride a bike. At first, you most likely stumbled a little and may have even fallen a few times. If you were using all-or-nothing thinking, you might have thoughts like:

"I'm either going to learn how to ride this perfectly, or I'm a complete failure."

"If I fall one more time, I'm never going to get it. I should just give up."

"Everyone else is better than me. The only person who can't do it is me.

Examples of all-or-nothing thinking include these ideas. They don't represent the reality of learning and are excessive. Learning requires practice, patience, and yes, some setbacks. It's not about being flawless at first. It's about making progress, even if it's only little steps.

All-or-nothing thinking can manifest itself in a variety of contexts, such as:

- School: "If I don't get an A on this test, I'm a failure."
- Sports: "If I don't score a goal, I'm letting my whole team down."
- Friendships: "If my friend doesn't agree with me on everything, they're not a true friend."
- Appearance:"If I don't look perfect, no one will like me."

Can you see how these all-or-nothing thoughts can cause negative emotions? If you feel that you must be flawless at all times, you're setting yourself up for disappointment? It can cause anxiety, stress, and even depression, as well as make you fear trying new things because you're afraid of failing?

Here are some other ways all-or-nothing thinking might show up:

- Success/Failure: Perceiving oneself as a complete failure or a full success, with no room for compromise.
- Good/Bad: Assigning a binary classification to oneself or others, disregarding any complexity or mixed attributes.
- Perfect/Imperfect: Using terms like "always" or "never" to describe circumstances, exaggerating their actuality
- Always/Never: Believing that anything less than perfect is unacceptable and a sign of failure.

Let's examine a few instances from actual life:

Consider Emily, a student engaged in a science project. She has worked very hard on it, but she is having trouble with one particular aspect. Thinking in terms of all or nothing, she would conclude, "This endeavor is a disaster! Everyone will think I'm dumb, and I'll receive a poor grade." She may become anxious, demoralized, and even tempted to abandon the endeavor entirely as a result of this way of thinking.

Here's another illustration: Consider David, a teenager, who is attempting to join the school's basketball team. Despite his skill as a player, he is anxious about the tryouts. "If I don't make the team, I'm a complete loser," he might think, thinking in terms of all or nothing. His performance during the tryouts may suffer as a result of this nervous way of thinking.

Let's now consider ways to counteract all-or-nothing thinking. Recognizing when you're slipping into this thought pattern is the first step. Are my perceptions of this circumstance limited to black and white? Am I utilizing phrases like "never" or "always"? Do I hold myself or others to a standard of perfection?

Once an all-or-nothing thought has been identified, look for evidence to the contrary. If you're thinking, "I always mess things up," for instance, consider instances in which you "didn't" make mistakes. There are many different levels of success and failure, so if you're thinking, "I'm either going to succeed completely, or I'm going to fail miserably," remind yourself that. You can ask yourself the following useful questions:

- Is there another perspective on this matter? How would I respond if a friend was experiencing this thought? Is my idea an exaggeration or is it entirely accurate?

- What could possibly go wrong? Is it truly that awful? * What is the best possible outcome?
- What is the most likely result?

Try this enjoyable hobby: Take a piece of paper and mark the center with a line. Jot down some of your recent all-or-nothing thoughts on one side. Conversely, jot down more practical and fair alternatives to such ideas. An alternative to "I'm a complete failure," for instance, would be "I made a mistake, but I can learn from it."

Making a "Shades of Gray" chart is an additional task you could attempt. On a sheet of paper, draw a line, marking one end "Completely Black" and the other "Completely White." Next, use various colors of gray to fill in the gaps.

Try to put a scenario on the chart where you frequently utilize all-or-nothing thinking. This can assist you in seeing the various options and avoiding too dramatic thinking.

A crucial first step in creating a more balanced and optimistic view of life is learning to question all-or-nothing thinking. It enables you to value your progress along the road, accept your flaws, and learn from your failures.

It's about accepting that both the world and we are complicated and multidimensional, and that's just acceptable! We'll examine catastrophizing, another typical thinking pitfall, and discover ways to prevent those "worst-case scenario" thoughts from taking control in the upcoming subchapter.

# CATASTROPHIZING: EXPECTING THE WORST

*"Worrying does not empty tomorrow of its sorrows, it empties today of its strength."* – Corrie ten Boom

Have you ever seen a terrifying movie and envisioned all sorts of bad things happening? Your heart races, your palms sweat, and you can scarcely watch. Your body responds as though the danger were real, even though it's only a movie. That's similar to catastrophizing, which is anticipating the worst even when there isn't any solid evidence that it will occur.

Understanding this typical thought trap and knowing how to prevent those "what if" concerns from gaining control are the main goals of this section. Imagine that a significant test is approaching. Even though you've done a lot of studying, you're still anxious. Your thoughts may sound something like this if you're catastrophizing:

- "What if the test is really hard and I fail?"
- "What if I lose my train of thought and forget everything I studied?"
- "What if everyone else does better than me and I look stupid?"

- "What if I fail the test and then I fail the whole class?"

All of these ideas are "what ifs"—concerns about situations that *might* occur but most likely won't. Catastrophizing is similar to mentally reenacting all the worst-case situations in a terrifying movie. Additionally, these thoughts can cause extreme anxiety and worry, much like watching a scary movie.

Catastrophizing can occur in a variety of contexts:

- School: "What if I give the wrong answer in class and everyone laughs at me?"
- Friendships: "What if my friend gets mad at me and never talks to me again?"
- Family: "What if my parents get sick and I have to take care of everyone?" The question, "What if I don't know anyone at the party and I feel awkward?" is relevant to social events.

Can you see how these awful thoughts can make you feel? They may cause anxiety, panic attacks, and even despair. They can also force you to stay away from circumstances that could cause these anxieties. For example, if you're afraid about making a presentation, you might try to get out of it altogether.

Here are some other ways catastrophizing might show up:

- Exaggerating the Issue: Making assumptions about the future without any solid evidence to back them up
- Jump to Conclusions: Ignoring any positive aspects of a situation and concentrating only on the possible negative outcomes; blowing a small problem out of proportion and imagining it to be much worse than it actually is.

A child named Sam, who has never attended a sleepover before and is a little anxious, might catastrophize by thinking, "What if I can't fall asleep and everyone makes fun of me?" or "What if I get homesick and have to call my parents in the middle of the night?" These thoughts could cause him to become so anxious that he chooses not to go at all. Let's look at some real-life examples.

Here's another illustration: Let's say Lisa, a teenager, is trying out for the school play. Although she has fantasized of performing on stage, she is also afraid of making a mistake in her lines. "What if I freeze up and forget all my lines?" or "What if I trip and fall on stage and everyone laughs at me?" are examples of catastrophizing.

She may become so anxious by these ideas that she decides not to try out for the play. How can we stop catastrophizing, then? Knowing when you're doing it is the first step. Consider this: Am I picturing the worst case scenario? Am I concentrating just on the bad? Am I speculating about what is ahead?

Here are some useful questions to ask you each time:

- What is the worst that "could" happen?
- What is the "most likely" outcome?
- What is the best that could happen?
- What are some other possible explanations for what might happen?
- If this did happen, what could I do to cope with it? Often, when we critically examine our worries, we discover that they are not as likely to occur as we think.
- You can ask yourself the following useful questions:
- What "could" possibly go wrong?
- What is the "likely" result?
- What is the best possible outcome?
- What other explanations might there be for what could occur?
- What could I do to deal with this if it did occur?

Fun activity: Think of your anxieties as airborne bubbles. Imagine popping the bubble and letting go of the concern when you catch yourself thinking something disastrous.

This can assist you in visualizing overcoming your worries.

Another thing you may do is make a "Worry Tree." Sketch a tree whose branches stand for many concerns. Note a "what if" scenario for each branch. Next, write a more reasonable and well-rounded solution next to each concern.

For instance, you may put "I've studied hard, and I'll do my best" in place of "What if I fail the test?" I can still gain knowledge even if I don't receive the grade I desire.

Building resilience and controlling anxiety can be achieved by learning to confront catastrophizing. It enables you to view situations more realistically and concentrate on the here and now rather than worrying about possible issues down the road.

It's about realizing that although horrible things can happen, they're usually not as bad as we think they would be and that we have the fortitude to handle any situation that arises. We'll examine personalizing, another typical thinking trap, and discover how to quit holding ourselves responsible for circumstances outside our control in the upcoming section.

## SELF-REFLECTION QUESTIONS

1.  Think about a recent situation where you felt upset or stressed. What thoughts went through your mind at the time?

    _____

    _____

    _____

2.  Can you identify any thinking traps that you might have fallen into during that situation? For example, were you catastrophizing or overgeneralizing?

    _____

    _____

    _____

3.  What are some of the most common thinking traps you tend to fall into?

    _____

    _____

    _____

4.  How do these thinking traps make you feel?

    _____

    _____

    _____

5. Can you think of a time when you successfully challenged a thinking trap? What did you do?

_____

_____

_____

## TRANSFORMATIVE EXERCISES

1. Thinking Trap Detective: Throughout the day, try to be a "thought detective" and notice when you're having negative thoughts. Ask yourself: Am I falling into any thinking traps? If so, which ones?

2. Thought Record: When you notice a negative thought, write it down. Then, ask yourself: Is this thought really true? What's the evidence for and against it? Is there another way to look at the situation? Try to reframe the thought into something more balanced and realistic.

3. "What If" Challenge: When you notice yourself catastrophizing ("What if...?" thoughts), ask yourself: What's the worst that "could" happen? What's the "most likely" outcome? What's the best that could happen? This can help you see things more realistically.

4. "Should" Statement Swap: When you notice yourself using "should" statements (e.g., "I should

be able to..."), try swapping them with "could" or "want to" statements. This can reduce pressure and guilt.

5. Positive Reframing: When you experience a setback or make a mistake, try to find something positive to focus on. What did you learn from the experience? How can you improve next time? This helps you develop resilience and a growth mindset.

# CHAPTER FIVE

# CHALLENGING NEGATIVE

# THOUGHTS: TURNING WOBBLES

# INTO STRENGTHS

---

*"The greatest weapon against stress is our ability to choose one thought over another."* – William James

Do you recall the shaky thoughts we discussed? The ones that leave you feeling uncertain, nervous, or a bit unsteady? They like tiny gremlins in your head, murmuring uncertainties and anxieties that may prevent you from moving on. However, what if you were able to control those gremlins and make those wobbles work to your advantage?

Giving you the skills to confront negative thoughts, transform them into more constructive ones, and increase your emotional resilience is the main goal of this chapter. Get into the mindset of a thought warrior now!

Let's consider a situation that is comparable. Consider a pupil by the name of Maya. She has been putting a lot of effort into a school assignment, but she is anxious about presenting it to the class. Her mind is racing with erratic ideas:

- "What if I mess up my presentation?"
- "What if everyone laughs at me?"
- "What if I forget everything I'm supposed to say?"

Negative thinking is exemplified by these "what if" scenarios. Although they aren't supported by any concrete data, they can cause Maya to become quite nervous and even consider skipping the presentation entirely. However, Maya is developing her ability to be a thought warrior. She's getting better at confronting those shaky ideas and using them to her advantage.

Recognizing when you're thinking negatively is the first step. It's similar like seeing those gremlins in the wild. Be mindful of your feelings. Are you depressed, anxious, or stressed? What are you thinking about, if you are? If you are able, put them in writing. This will make you more conscious of the way you think. It's time to don your thought warrior armor and confront any bad thoughts you've discovered. Pose some challenging questions to yourself:

- Is this idea actually accurate? What are the arguments in favor of and against it?
- Is there another perspective on this matter?

- How would I respond if a friend was experiencing this thought?
- Am I overstating the issue?
- Am I making assumptions too quickly?

**Let us return to Maya's presentation. Despite her shaky ideas, she is prepared to confront them. The question, "What if I mess up my presentation?" crossed my mind.**

- Difficulty: "I am familiar with the content and have rehearsed this presentation. It won't be disastrous even if I make a minor error. Everybody makes errors from time to time. The thought that crossed my mind was, "What if everyone laughs at me?"
- Difficulty: "I doubt that everyone will find it funny. The majority of individuals are helpful. Furthermore, it is not my problem if a small number of individuals do find it funny. I'll concentrate on giving it my all."
- Thought: "What if I forget everything I'm supposed to say?"
- Difficulty: "I've made notes to aid with my memory of the main ideas. And I can probably figure it out as I go along, even if I do forget something. I'm flexible and resourceful."

Observe how Maya is transforming those erratic thoughts into more realistic and upbeat ones. She is not acting as though there is no chance of anything going wrong. She's only reminding herself of her talents and abilities and choosing to see the bright side.

Other techniques to combat negative thinking include the following:

- Reframe the thought: Take a fresh look at the circumstance. Instead of thinking, "I failed the test," for instance, you can consider, "I didn't do as well as I hoped, but I can learn from my mistakes and do better next time."
- Look for the bright side: There is usually a tiny silver lining, even in the most trying circumstances. Look for it. For instance, you may have developed your skills and gained new friends during the tryouts even if you are not selected for the squad.
- Make use of humor: Laughing at our own anxieties can sometimes de-escalate them. Look for the humor in the circumstance.

Speak with a trustworthy person: Talking to a friend, relative, or responsible adult about your concerns might help you get perspective and support.

Try this enjoyable hobby:    Make your own "Thought Warrior Shield." Draw a shield and adorn it with representations of your virtues and strong points. Imagine raising your shield to block out bad thoughts when they arise. One more thing you may do is make a "Positive Affirmations Jar." On pieces of paper, write affirmations such as "I am capable,""I am strong," or "I am kind." Take a slip of paper out of the jar and read it to yourself whenever you're feeling low.

Keep in mind that confronting negative ideas is a skill that requires repetition. It will get easier the more you do it. It's similar to picking up a new sport. It may feel awkward and challenging at first, but you will gain confidence and skill with practice.

One of the most effective ways to improve your mental health is to learn how to control your erratic thoughts and use them to your advantage. It's about realizing that your thoughts greatly influence your feelings and actions, and that you have the ability to select them. We'll discover even more amazing methods for regulating your emotions and developing resilience in the upcoming chapter.

# THOUGHT RECORDS: YOUR DETECTIVE TOOLKIT FOR CHALLENGING THOUGHTS

*"The most important thing is this: to be able at any moment to sacrifice what we are for what we could become."* – Charles Dickens

Consider yourself a detective looking into a mystery. To solve the case, you would collect hints, examine the evidence, and put the pieces together, right? Well, sometimes your thoughts are also a mystery! They appear in your thoughts, impacting your emotions and behavior, but you may not always know their origins or whether they are accurate.

This introduces you to the Thought Record, a mental detective toolbox. It's an effective technique that can assist you in exploring your thoughts, confronting pessimistic ideas, and eventually taking control of your mental health.

Imagine that you are about to take a significant test. You've put a lot of effort into your studies, but your anxiety persists. Concerns are rushing through your head: "What if I blank out?""What if I fail?""What if everyone else does better than me?" You're feeling anxious and may even want to stop studying entirely because of these "what if" scenarios.

The Thought Record enters the picture here. A straightforward yet powerful tool for better understanding your thoughts and emotions is the Thought Record. It functions similarly to a worksheet, with various columns that help you recognize, examine, and confront bad beliefs. A Thought Record usually looks like this:

1.  Situation: Explain the circumstance that led to the negative thought. Give specifics. What took place? Who took part? You were where? For instance: "I was sitting in class waiting for the test to start."

2.  Automatic Thoughts: These are the ideas that immediately came to mind when you were in that circumstance. They frequently happen quickly and reflexively. Even if your thoughts appear absurd or illogical, put them in writing. As an illustration, "I'm going to fail this test.""Everyone else is going to do better than me."

3.  Emotions: List the feelings you felt in that circumstance. Give specifics. Did you experience fear, anxiety, sadness, anger, or another emotion? On a scale of 0 to 100, indicate how intense the emotion is (0 being not at all, 100 being the most intense). For example: "Anxious (80)."

4.  Supporting Information for the Negative Thought: What facts back up your negative thought? Be

truthful with yourself. As an illustration, "I've failed tests before.""I sometimes have trouble remembering information under pressure."

5. Evidence Disproving the Negative Theory: Which facts refute the bad thought you have? Which viewpoints are more realistic or upbeat? As an illustration, "I've studied really hard for this test.""I've done well on other tests in this class.""Even if I don't get a perfect score, it's not the end of the world."

6. Alternative Thought: What is a more realistic and balanced way of looking at the situation in light of the facts you have gathered? This should be a less negative and more beneficial thought. For instance: "I'm going to give this test my best effort because I'm well-prepared for it. I can still gain knowledge even if I don't receive the grade I desire.

7. .Result: After confronting your negative notion, how did you feel and behave? Did your anxiety level drop? More assured? Have you changed anything? For instance: "I felt much more concentrated and at ease. I managed to focus on the test and give it my all.

Let's examine another illustration. Consider Jake, a teenager who is depressed since his friend called off their planned hangout.

1. Circumstance: "I received a text from a friend stating that he was unable to spend today with me."
2. . Automated Ideas: "He doesn't want to spend time with me anymore.""I must have done something wrong.""No one likes me."
3. Emotions: Lonely (85), Sad (90)
4. Supporting information for the negative opinion: "He's been acting a little distant lately."
5. Proof Contrary to the Negative Thought: "He's been really busy with schoolwork lately.""He said he was sorry he had to cancel.""He suggested we hang out another time."
6. Different Perspective: "It's likely that he's simply really busy. He had to cancel, but that's all right. Later, when he's free, I'll text him."
7. Result: Less depressed and isolated. I texted my pal to arrange things for the next week.

See how Jake was able to confront his bad ideas and feel better by using the Thought Record? It helps you discover the truth about your thoughts and feelings, much like a detective toolbox for your mind.

Try this enjoyable hobby: Make a worksheet for your personal Thought Record. You can make a table on a computer or sketch the columns on paper. Have a few copies of the worksheet on hand, and if you find yourself thinking negatively, take it out and complete it.

Using Thought Records to role-play with a friend or relative is an additional activity you can attempt. Assist one another in completing the Thought Record by taking turns describing circumstances that make you think negatively. One effective method for developing emotional resilience is the Thought Record. It assists you in:

- Be more cognizant of what you're thinking: You can become more conscious of your thought patterns and see recurring negative themes by putting your ideas in writing.

- Challenge pessimistic thoughts: You can view your negative thoughts more objectively by using the Thought Record, which offers an organized method of analyzing the evidence for and against them.

- Create a more balanced way of thinking: By identifying different viewpoints, you can swap out pessimistic beliefs for more practical and beneficial ones.

- Emotional well-being: By altering your thoughts, you can alter your feelings and behaviors, which will increase your emotional well-being.

It's like discovering a new superpower when you learn how to use Thought Records. It enables you to take charge of your ideas and emotions and build a happier, more satisfying existence. We'll look at behavioral experiments, another effective technique for controlling your emotions, in the upcoming subchapter.

# REFRAMING: CHANGING NEGATIVE THOUGHTS INTO MORE BALANCED ONES

*"We cannot direct the wind, but we can adjust the sails."*
– Dolly Parton

Consider yourself at the helm of a vessel. The events in your life are symbolized by the wind; on some days it is strong and pleasant, but on other days it is feeble or blowing in the wrong direction. Just like you can't always control what occurs to you, you can't control the wind.

However, the way you change your sails is something that you "can" manage.

In order to handle life's ups and downs with more ease and confidence, this subchapter focuses on learning to modify your "thought sails"—that is, to take those negative ideas that are throwing you off course and reframe them into something more balanced and beneficial.

Let's consider a typical situation. Consider that you are both anxious and thrilled about a school dance. "What if no one dances with me?" is one of the negative ideas that could begin to seep in. "What if I trip and fall in front of everyone?" "What if I look awkward and everyone makes fun of me?" You may feel quite nervous and maybe consider skipping the dance entirely as a result of these ideas.

Reframing is the process of taking those pessimistic ideas and rephrasing them to reflect a different perspective. Pretending that you're not anxious or that nothing negative might occur is not the point. It's about confronting those "what if" concerns and gaining a more realistic and balanced viewpoint.

You can change your negative dance ideas by doing the following:

- "What if no one dances with me?" is a negative thought that comes to mind.

- Reframe: It's probable that not everyone will ask me to dance, but that's good too. Dancing with friends or by myself is still enjoyable for me. And who knows, I might get an unexpected question from someone!"

- "What if I trip and fall in front of everyone?" is a negative thought.
- Reframe: "Mistakes are inevitable for everyone. I'll just laugh it off and continue dancing if I trip. The world won't end because of it.
- "What if I look awkward and everyone makes fun of me?" is a negative thought.
- Reframe: "I'm going to concentrate on enjoying myself and having fun. It's okay if I feel a little uncomfortable. Everyone has such moments. Furthermore, it speaks more about the person than it does about me if they make fun of me.

Do you see how those reframed ideas are more sensible and beneficial? They stress your capacity to manage any situation that arises, but also acknowledging the chance that things won't go exactly as planned.

They provide you the ability to take control of your experience and concentrate on the things that you "can" control, such as your behavior and attitude.

**Other techniques for reframing include the following**:

- Challenge the evidence: Consider this: What is the real proof for this unfavorable opinion? Is it merely an assumption or is it supported by facts? When we look attentively at our negative thoughts, we frequently find that they are not as strong as we believe.

- Think about additional possibilities: What other explanations might there be for the circumstance? We frequently assume the worst without taking into account other, more plausible scenarios.

- Contextualize it: Does this matter as much as it appears to be right now? In a week, will it really matter that much? In a month? By keeping things in perspective, we can prevent ourselves from exaggerating minor issues.

- Pay attention to what you can control: Pay attention to what you *can* control, such as your thoughts, feelings, and actions, rather than worrying about things that are beyond your control.

Let's examine a few more instances from actual life when reframing can be beneficial: Consider Ben, a student, who receives a poor score on an exam. "I'm so stupid," may have been his first thinking. I will never be proficient in this subject.

However, he may reframe it as follows: "All right, I didn't do as well as I had hoped. It's only one test, though. I may speak with the instructor, determine my areas of weakness, and put in more effort the next time.

Here's another illustration: Consider Sarah, a teenager, and her best friend arguing. She may have thought at first, "She despises me." We are no longer buddies. She may, however, reframe it as follows: "We're both upset right now. It will likely take us a while to calm off. However, we have previously had problems and always managed to work things out." 9

Try this enjoyable hobby: Make a worksheet called "Reframing Worksheet." On a sheet of paper, draw a line through the center. Write a bad thought on one side. Write a revised, more impartial version of the idea on the opposite side.

An additional activity that you could try is "Reframing Charades." A scenario that could elicit a negative thought is acted out by one person. After guessing the scenario, the other person must reframe any potential negative thoughts associated with it. Reframing negative ideas is a useful skill that can assist you in:

- Decrease tension and anxiety: You might feel more at ease and in control of your emotions by confronting negative thoughts.

- Uplift your spirits: By changing your attention from negative to positive, reframing can help you feel happier and have a more optimistic view.

- Build resilience: You will be more resilient and better able to manage obstacles in the future if you learn how to overcome failures.

- Increase your self-confidence: Reframing can assist you in identifying your own talents and capabilities, which will result in a greater sense of self-worth and confidence.

The ability to change your ideas and emotions through reframing is similar to possessing a superpower. It's an effective tool for enhancing emotional health and making life happier and more satisfying. We'll look at behavioral experiments, another crucial technique for controlling your emotions, in the upcoming subchapter.

## SELF-REFLECTION QUESTIONS

1. Think about a recent situation where you had a strong negative emotion (like anxiety or sadness). What were the thoughts that went through your head at that time?

_____

_____

_____

2. Can you identify any patterns in your negative thinking? Do you tend to worry about the same kinds of things?

_____

_____

_____

3. When you have a negative thought, what are some of the first things you usually do or tell yourself?

_____

_____

_____

4. How do your negative thoughts affect your behavior? Do they make you avoid certain situations or people?

_____

_____

_____

5. What are some things you can tell yourself to challenge your negative thoughts and make them more balanced or positive?

_____

_____

_____

## TRANSFORMATIVE EXERCISES

1. Thought-Stopping: When you notice a negative thought, say "Stop!" (either out loud or in your head). This can help interrupt the flow of negative thinking. Then, replace the negative thought with a more positive or neutral one.

2. Thought-Challenging Questions: When you have a negative thought, ask yourself: Is this thought really true? What's the evidence for and against it? Is there another way to look at the situation? What would I tell a friend who was having this thought?

3. Positive Affirmations: Create a list of positive statements about yourself (e.g., "I am capable,""I am strong,""I am kind"). Read these affirmations to yourself regularly, especially when you're struggling with negative thoughts.

4. "What If" Reframe: When you're worrying about "what if" scenarios (catastrophizing), ask yourself: What's the worst that "could" happen? What's the "most likely" outcome? What's the best that could

happen? This can help you see things more realistically.

5. Thought Diary: Keep a journal where you write down negative thoughts, the feelings they trigger, and then reframe those thoughts into more balanced or positive ones. This helps you track your progress and see how your thinking changes over time.

# CHAPTER SIX

# CONQUERING YOUR FEARS: STEPPING OUTSIDE YOUR COMFORT ZONE

*"The cave you fear to enter holds the treasure you seek."*
– Joseph Campbell

Have you ever had the feeling that a large, menacing spider is lying in the corner of your room, or that a tiny monster is hiding beneath your bed? Fear can be extremely strong emotions that cause your heart to race, your hands to perspire, and your stomach to turn over. However, what if you were able to master those anxieties and transform them from terrifying monsters into doable obstacles?

This chapter focuses on overcoming your concerns, venturing outside of your comfort zone, and realizing your incredible potential. It's time to start fighting fear!

Let's consider a widespread phobia that many children and teenagers have: the dread of public speaking. Let's say you are required to present in class. Your mouth becomes dry, your heart begins to race, and you may even have mild vertigo. "What if" scenarios are racing through your head: "What if I forget my lines?" "What if everyone laughs at me?""What if I mess up the whole thing?" These emotions are quite typical. An instinctive human reaction, fear serves to keep us safe from harm.

However, occasionally our brains might overreact, causing the fear response to be triggered even in the absence of a genuine threat. This is the case with social circumstances, test anxiety, and public speaking. The worry is genuine but the danger isn't.

So, how can we overcome these fears? The secret is to expose yourself to your fears gradually, under supervision, and in a safe manner. It's similar to learning how to swim. You wouldn't immediately dive into the deep end of the pool, would you? Starting in the shallow end, you would gradually move deeper as you become more accustomed to the water. Overcoming fears is comparable. It involves gradually stepping beyond of your comfort zone and gaining confidence in the process.

**Here's a methodical way to overcome your fears**:

1. Determine what you are frightened of: What is it? Give specifics. Is it speaking in front of an audience? Speaking with strangers? Are you attempting to join a sports team? Without training wheels, are you riding your bike?

2. Make a fear ladder: Divide your fear into more manageable, smaller steps. Work your way up to the most difficult scenario by starting with something that is only mildly frightening. Your fear ladder might resemble this, for instance, if you're terrified of public speaking:

- Discussing your project with one friend.
- Using a mirror to practice your presentation.
- Making your family a presentation. Introducing oneself to a select set of friends.
- Giving a presentation to the entire class.

3. Get started modestly: Start with the step on your fear ladder that is the simplest. Avoid taking on too much at once. Before proceeding to the following phase, the objective is to progressively become accustomed to each one.

4. Regular practice: The more you encounter the things that frighten you, the less frightening they will seem. Make it a point to routinely practice every stage on your fear ladder.

5. Reward yourself: Acknowledge your accomplishments as you go. Give yourself a pat on the back every time you reach the top of your fear

ladder. This will support your continued motivation and progress.

6. Remain persistent: You will have moments of fear or discouragement. It's alright. Just remember to keep practicing.

Let's examine some actual instances of children and teenagers overcoming their fears: Consider a little child named Alex who has a dog phobia. This is how his fear ladder may appear:

- Seeing images of dogs.
- Seeing videos of dogs.
- Being across the street from a leashed dog.
- Getting closer to a leashed dog.
- Petting a leash-wearing, little, amiable dog.
- Playing in a park with a dog.

Alex can conquer his fear of dogs by progressively climbing the ladder.

Here's another illustration. Consider Sarah, a teenager who fears social situations. This is how her fear ladder may appear:

- Greeting a person in the corridor.
- Striking up a discussion with a student.
- Participating in an activity or club.
- Joining a friend for a celebration.

- Attending a party on her own.

Sarah can overcome her anxiety of social situations and increase her social confidence by taking little steps outside of her comfort zone.

Try this enjoyable hobby:  For whatever you're frightened of, make your own fear ladder. Describe each step in detail and make it as easy as you can.

Locating a friend who has a similar fear is an additional activity you can attempt. Together, you may overcome your worries, supporting and motivating one another as you go. It's a journey, not a race, to overcome your worries.

It requires guts, patience, and time. However, the benefits are unquestionably worthwhile. You'll learn new things about yourself, gain confidence, and access a world of opportunities by venturing outside of your comfort zone. We'll discover some awesome methods for controlling our anxiousness and maintaining composure under pressure in the upcoming chapter.

## UNDERSTANDING FEAR AND ANXIETY: WHAT HAPPENS IN YOUR BODY?

*"Fear is only as deep as the mind allows."* – Japanese Proverb

When you're afraid or nervous, have you ever had the feeling that your body is acting independently? Your palms begin to perspire, your heart begins to race, and you may even get butterflies in your stomach. Even when there isn't any actual threat, it feels like your body is pressing the panic button. The main focus of this subchapter is learning about the physiological reactions to worry and fear. It's like having a backstage pass to your inner workings, allowing you to learn how to take charge and comprehend why you feel the way you do.

Consider a moment when you were ecstatic about something, such as riding a roller coaster. You may have had a slight flutter in your stomach, sweating hands, and an accelerated heartbeat.

Those bodily feelings are very comparable to those experienced during anxiety or fear. The "reason" for such feelings is where the difference lies. It's the thrill of the trip on the roller coaster. Your body is preparing you for a perceived threat when you are experiencing fear.

Imagine coming upon a snake while out for a walk in the woods. The snake is immediately interpreted by your brain as a possible threat. Your body receives a signal from it that sets off the "fight-or-flight" reaction. To prepare you to either flee or protect yourself, your heart begins to beat more quickly in order to pump more blood to your muscles.

Your breathing quickens in order to supply your body with more oxygen. Your tense muscles prepare you for action. In an attempt to cool off, you may even begin to perspire. Your nervous system, a sophisticated network of nerves that send signals throughout your body, regulates all of these physical changes. Your nervous system goes into overdrive when you're afraid or anxious, releasing substances like adrenaline that triggers those physical sensations.

**Here are some frequent bodily indicators of fear and anxiety:**

- Increased heart rate
- Rapid breathing
- Sweaty palms
- Muscle tension
- Stomachache or nausea
- Headache
- Dizziness
- Trembling or shaking
- Dry mouth

It is crucial to keep in mind that these physical sensations are typical. They are your body's method of getting ready to handle a perceived danger. But occasionally, when there isn't any actual danger, our brains might become too sensitive and start the fight-or-flight reaction. That is the case with conditions like phobias, test anxiety, and social anxiety.

Let's take a closer look at how the brain contributes to anxiety and fear. The amygdala is a tiny region in the brain that functions as your brain's alarm system, identifying threats and triggering the fear response. When the amygdala detects danger, it sends signals to other parts of your brain and body, resulting in the physical symptoms we discussed.

However, occasionally, the amygdala can be a bit too sensitive, setting off the alarm even when there isn't a real threat, which can cause feelings of panic and anxiety. It's like having a smoke alarm that goes off every time you burn toast!

It can be quite beneficial to understand how the body and brain respond to worry and terror. Realizing that such bodily feelings are simply your body's typical reaction to stress can be helpful. They don't indicate that there is a major problem.

Let's examine some actual instances of how children and teenagers deal with anxiety and fear: Consider a little child named Michael who has a dog phobia. His amygdala activates, causing the fight-or-flight reaction, when he spots a dog. His palms begin to perspire, his heart begins to race, and he may even feel like fleeing. For Michael, these bodily symptoms can be quite frightening and exacerbate his dog phobia.

Here's another illustration: Consider Sarah, a teenager who experiences severe anxiety prior to presenting presentations in class. The "threat" of public speaking is perceived by her amygdala, which sets off the fear response. She may have a beating heart, shaking hands, and a dry mouth. Her dread of public speaking may be exacerbated by these physical symptoms, which may make it even more difficult for her to deliver her presentation.

Try this enjoyable hobby: A "Body Scan" chart should be made. Label the various bodily parts (head, chest, stomach, hands, etc.) in a drawing of a body. Consider a moment when you experienced fear or anxiety. Where did you sense the sensations in your body? Did your chest feel constricted? You have a knot in your stomach? On your Body Scan chart, highlight those areas. This can help you become more aware of how your body reacts to fear and worry.

There are a variety of deep breathing techniques that you can try, but one basic method is to inhale slowly through your nose, hold your breath for a few seconds, and then exhale slowly through your mouth. Deep breathing exercises can also help to calm your nervous system and lessen the physical symptoms of anxiety and fear.

One of the most important steps in learning to control your anxiety and dread is realizing how your mind and body interact. It helps you understand that those bodily symptoms are not an indication that you're losing control, but rather are a typical reaction to stress. The following subchapter will cover some useful techniques for reducing anxiety and fear's physical manifestations and relaxing your nervous system.

# GRADUAL EXPOSURE: TAKING SMALL

# STEPS TO FACE YOUR FEARS

*"Courage is not the absence of fear, but the triumph over it."* – Nelson Mandela

Envision learning how to ride a bicycle. Attempting to ride down a steep hill would not be your first move, would it? Most likely, you would begin in a park or a peaceful street, possibly even with training wheels. You would start off slowly, gain confidence with time, and become accustomed to balance. This is precisely how overcoming anxieties is accomplished through progressive exposure. It involves facing your concerns by taking tiny, doable measures and gradually increasing your bravery and self-assurance. Learning how to apply this effective strategy to get over your fears is the main focus of this subchapter.

Let's consider a widespread phobia that many children and teenagers have: the dread of public speaking. Let's say you are required to present in class. Just the thought of standing up in front of everyone and talking can make your heart race and your palms sweat. You might even start having those "what if" worries:

- "What if I forget my lines?"
- "What if everyone laughs at me?"
- "What if I mess up the whole thing?"

These emotions are perfectly normal. Fear is a normal human reaction, but occasionally our brains can become overly protective and set off the fear response even when there isn't a real threat.

This is the case with social situations, public speaking, and test anxiety, for example. Gradual exposure helps you retrain your brain by demonstrating to it that the things you're afraid of aren't as dangerous as you believe. It's like teaching your brain a new trick: you start with something that's a little frightening and work your way up to the most difficult scenario.

**The process of progressive exposure is as follows:**

1. Determine what you are frightened of: What is it? Give specifics. Is it speaking in front of an audience? Speaking with strangers? Are you attempting to join a sports team? Without training wheels, are you riding your bike?
2. Make a fear ladder: Divide your fear into more manageable, smaller steps. Work your way up to the most difficult scenario by starting with something that is only mildly frightening. Your fear ladder might resemble this, for instance, if you're terrified of public speaking:
    - Thinking about the presentation.
    - Rehearsing your presentation in your room by yourself.

- Using a mirror to practice your presentation.
- Making your family a presentation.
- Introducing oneself to a select set of friends.
- Giving a presentation to the entire class.

3. Take the first step on your fear ladder that is the simplest. Avoid taking on too much at once. Before proceeding to the following phase, the objective is to progressively become accustomed to each one.

4. Repeat and practice: The more you encounter the things that frighten you, the less frightening they will seem. Make it a point to practice every step on your fear ladder until it becomes easier.

5. Remain with it: You may have the impulse to retreat or completely flee the situation when you're facing your anxiety. It's critical to fight this temptation and endure it until your worry begins to subside. It could take a few minutes or more, however the more time you spend, the faster your fear will subside.

6. Reward yourself by acknowledging your accomplishments along the road. Give yourself a pat on the back every time you reach the top of

your fear ladder. This will support your continued motivation and progress.

Let's examine some actual instances of how children and teenagers can get over their concerns through steady exposure: Consider Kevin, a young child who has a dog phobia. This is how his fear ladder may appear:

- Seeing images of dogs.
- Seeing videos of dogs.
- Being across the street from a leashed dog.
- Getting closer to a leashed dog.
- Petting a leash-wearing, little, amiable dog.
- Playing in a park with a dog.

By gradually working his way up the ladder, Kevin can learn to manage his fear of dogs. Here's another illustration. Imagine a teen named Maria who's afraid of social situations. This is how her fear ladder may appear:

- Greeting a person in the corridor.
- Striking up a discussion with a student.
- Participating in an activity or club.
- Joining a friend for a celebration.
- Attending a party on her own.
- By taking small steps outside her comfort zone, Maria can build her social confidence and reduce her anxiety in social settings.

Try this enjoyable hobby: **Think about something you're afraid of and create your own fear ladder. Describe each step in detail and make it as easy as you can.**

Locating a friend who has a similar fear is an additional activity you can attempt. Together, you may overcome your worries, supporting and motivating one another as you go. Remember, overcoming fears is a journey, not a race. It requires guts, patience, and time. However, the benefits are unquestionably worthwhile.

By employing incremental exposure, you can learn to manage your fear, increase your confidence, and open up a world of new possibilities. We'll look at some more methods for controlling anxiety and maintaining composure under pressure in the upcoming section.

## SELF-REFLECTION QUESTIONS

1.  What are some of the things you're most afraid of?

    _____

    _____

    _____

2.  How do your fears affect your life? Do they prevent you from doing things you want to do?

    _____

    _____

    _____

3. When you think about facing your fears, what are the thoughts that go through your head?

_____

_____

_____

4. Have you ever tried to face a fear before? What was that experience like?

_____

_____

_____

5. What are some small steps you could take to start facing one of your fears?

_____

_____

_____

## TRANSFORMATIVE EXERCISES

1. Create a Fear Ladder: Choose one of your fears and break it down into smaller, less scary steps. Start with the least anxiety-provoking step and gradually work your way up to the most challenging.

2. "BRAVE" Plan: Use the acronym BRAVE to create a plan for facing your fear:

1. "B"reak it down: Divide your fear into small steps.

2. "R"elax: Practice relaxation techniques (deep breathing, mindfulness) before and during exposure.

3. "A"ssess: Rate your anxiety level before, during, and after each exposure.

4. "V"ary: Try different ways of facing your fear.

5. "E"njoy: Reward yourself for your progress.

3. Exposure Practice: Regularly practice the steps on your fear ladder. Start with the easiest step and repeat it until it feels less scary. Then, move on to the next step.

4. Visualization: Imagine yourself successfully facing your fear. Visualize the situation in detail, focusing on how you will feel calm and confident.

5. Challenge Negative Thoughts: When you notice negative thoughts about your fear (e.g., "I can't do this,""I'm going to mess up"), challenge those thoughts. Ask yourself: Are these thoughts really true? Is there another way to look at the situation? Replace negative thoughts with more positive and realistic ones.

# CHAPTER SEVEN

# TAMING YOUR TEMPER: MANAGING ANGER IN HEALTHY WAYS

---

*"Anger is like electricity. It's powerful, and if used wisely it lights the way. If abused, it will kill."* – Theodore Rubin

Have you ever had the feeling of a volcano erupting? Your face becoming hot, your muscles tensing up, or that burning sensation in your chest are all indicators that your temper is raising. Anger is a strong emotion that, if not controlled, may be destructive, much like a volcano. However, we can learn to control our temper and deal with anger in constructive ways, just as we can learn to harness the power of electricity.

Understanding anger, identifying its triggers, and creating healthy coping mechanisms are the main topics of this chapter. It's time to manage your rage!

Let's consider a typical scenario that can make children and teenagers angry: feeling like they're being treated unfairly. Imagine feeling as though one of your friends is cheating while you're playing a game with them. You might start to feel frustrated, then irritated, and finally, downright angry. Your thoughts might be racing: "That's not fair!""He's always cheating!""I'm going to get him back!" These feelings are understandable. It's natural to feel angry when you perceive injustice.

But how you express that rage might make all the difference. You could yell at your friend, accuse him of cheating, and storm off in a huff. Alternatively, you could take a deep breath, attempt to relax, and then calmly explain your feelings about his infidelity.

Your initial response may provide a momentary sensation of relief, but it may also intensify the conflict and cause damaged sentiments. Even while it can require more work at the time, the second response has a higher chance of producing a favorable outcome.

Anger, like happiness, sorrow, or fear, is a normal human emotion. It isn't necessarily "bad." Anger may actually be a strong motivation that helps us set limits, defend our rights, and improve our lives. When anger is released in inappropriate ways, such as yelling, hostility, or violence, it becomes a problem.

These are a few typical things that make people angry: Feeling mistreated, being judged or ridiculed, not receiving what you want, being ignored or disrespected, feeling frustrated or disappointed, seeing injustice in action, or feeling intimidated or dangerous Everyone experiences anger differently.

Some people could get physically upset, while others might become silent and withdrawn. Anger can be openly expressed by some people or kept inside by others. Anger is a feeling that can be expressed in any form. Finding healthy ways to deal with it is crucial. Physical indicators that your temper is raising include the following:

- Increased heart rate
- Rapid breathing
- Muscle tension
- Clenched fists
- Flushed face
- Sweating
- Headache
- Stomachache

Being able to identify these bodily indicators is similar to having an early warning system. It provides you with an opportunity to act before your rage become unmanageable. The following are some constructive methods for handling anger:

- **Inhale deeply**: You can lessen the severity of your rage and relax your nervous system by taking deep breaths. Try taking a slow, deep breath with your nose, holding it for a few seconds, and then letting it out through your mouth slowly. Let's count to ten: This time-tested method can assist in allowing you to take a minute to reflect before acting. Additionally, it can assist in diverting your attention from your furious thoughts.

- **Have a rest**: Take some time away from the issue if your anger is getting the better of you. Find a peaceful location where you can gather your thoughts.

- **Calmly and assertively express your feelings**: Try to calmly and assertively communicate your feelings when you've cooled down. To express your feelings without placing blame or criticizing the other person, use "I" words. Rather than shouting, "You cheated!" for instance, you could say, "I feel frustrated because it seems like the rules weren't being followed."

- **Find healthy outlets for your anger**: Take part in artistic endeavors, sports, or physical activity that helps you blow off steam.

- **Speak with a trustworthy person**: You can process your anger and acquire perspective by talking to a friend, relative, or responsible adult about how you're feeling.

Let's examine some actual instances of how children and teenagers can control their anger: Consider Ben, a young child who is upset because his younger sibling is constantly damaging his toys. Ben could calmly communicate his feelings after taking a deep breath and counting to ten, rather than shouting at his sibling. Additionally, he may find constructive ways to deal with his anger, such as painting or going for a run.

Here's another illustration: Consider a teenager named Sarah who is upset that she was left off of the school's cheer team. Sarah should discuss her displeasure with a trusted person rather than snapping at her friends or family. She might also do things that bring her joy, such as spending time with her pets or listening to music.

Try this enjoyable hobby: Establish a "Anger Thermometer." Label several areas of a thermometer with varying degrees of rage, ranging from "Calm" to "Raging." Try to determine where you are on the thermometer when you begin to feel angry. This can assist you in acting before your rage becomes more intense.

An additional task you could do is to construct a "Coping Skills Toolbox." Stuff a box with things that help you deal with your anger, such as coloring books, stress balls, or journals. You can use a tool from your toolbox to assist you relax if you're feeling upset.

Building emotional wellbeing and wholesome relationships requires the ability to control one's anger. It involves identifying your triggers, comprehending your bodily reactions, and creating healthy coping mechanisms for your anger. We'll look at how to develop resilience and overcome setbacks in the upcoming chapter.

## RECOGNIZING YOUR ANGER TRIGGERS: WHAT MAKES YOU MAD?

*"Anyone can become angry – that is easy, but to be angry with the right person and to the right degree and at the right time and for the right purpose and in the right way – that is not easy."* – Aristotle

Consider yourself a detective attempting to crack a case. Getting hints is the first step, isn't it? You must comprehend the events, the parties involved, and the possible causes of the predicament. In fact, controlling one's wrath is somewhat similar to detective work.

Knowing what makes you angry and what "clues" make you lose your temper is the first step. Being a "feelings detective" and identifying your anger triggers are the main topics of this subchapter. It's similar to getting to know your inner villains so you can predict their actions and prevent them from creating too much problems.

Let's consider a relatable example: let's say you're playing a video game and are about to beat your high score when your younger sibling interrupts you, accidentally turning the game off. How would you feel? You could probably pretty frustrated, maybe even angry, right? That interruption and that particular situation are potential anger triggers.

An anger trigger is anything that makes you angry; it could be a person, a place, a situation, or even a thought. It's like a button that gets pressed, causing your anger to surface. The first step to effectively managing your anger is identifying your triggers.

**The following are some typical types of rage triggers:**

- **Situations**: Particular incidents or situations that aggravate you. Examples include losing a match, receiving a poor grade, receiving public criticism, and having something taken from you without your consent.

- **People**: Specific people whose words or behaviors frequently make you feel agitated or angry. Examples include a buddy who betrays their commitments, a sibling who taunts you, or a classmate who bullies you.

- **Thoughts**: Unhelpful or negative thought patterns that make you angry. For instance, "It's not fair!""He's always doing this to me!""I can't stand it!"

- **Internal Events**: Emotional or physical conditions that may increase your proneness to rage. Examples include being exhausted, hungry, anxious, ill, or feeling other intense emotions like grief or anxiety.

It's critical to keep in mind that every person has unique anger triggers. Something that irritates one individual may not bother another at all. When it comes to anger triggers, there is no right or wrong answer. Finding *your* unique triggers is crucial.

Let's examine some actual instances of what makes children and teenagers angry: Consider David, a student who becomes quickly irritated when he perceives unjust treatment. Other children cutting in front of him or feeling like a teacher is being overly severe with him could be triggers for him.

Here's another illustration: Consider a teenager named Sarah who becomes upset when she is treated disrespectfully or neglected. She may become triggered when someone talks down to her or when her friends make plans without consulting her. Some common categories of anger triggers include the following:

- **Situations**: Specific events or circumstances that make you angry. A few instances are losing a game, getting a bad grade, being criticized in public, and having something taken away from you without your permission.

- **People**: Particular individuals whose actions or statements regularly cause you to feel annoyed or furious. Examples include a classmate who bullies you, a sibling who taunts you, or a friend who breaks their promises.

- **Thoughts**: Negative or unhelpful thought patterns that aggravate you. Take "It's not fair!" as an example. "He's always doing this to me!" "I can't stand it!"

Try this enjoyable hobby: A "My Anger Triggers" chart should be made. Create a chart with the following four columns: Internal Event, Situation, Person, and Thought. Keep an eye out for moments throughout the day when you feel angry. Try to identify what triggered your anger and write it down in the appropriate column. This can help you spot patterns in your rage triggers.

Another activity you might attempt is to keep an "Anger Diary." Whenever you sense rage, write down the following information:

- Time and date: When did the outburst of rage happen?

- Context: What took place? Give specifics.

- Triggers: What particular individuals, ideas, or inner circumstances triggered your rage?

- Physical signs: What bodily symptoms, such as clinched fists or a pounding heart, did you observe?

- Intensity: On a scale of 1 to 10, how furious were you?

- How you responded: When you were upset, what did you say or do? You can monitor your anger triggers and spot trends over time by keeping an anger diary.

It's also beneficial to consider the early indicators of anger. These are the subtle signs that you are becoming angry. They could be emotional, like a sense of annoyance, or physical, like a tiny tenseness in your shoulders. You may be able to take action before your anger erupts if you can identify these early warning indicators.

The following are some typical early indicators of anger: An elevated heart rate, fast breathing, tense muscles, a clenched jaw or fists, a flushed face, and a restless or unsettled feeling. It's like having a superpower when you learn to identify your anger triggers and warning indicators. It enables you to foresee potential triggers for your anger and take action to regulate it before it becomes unmanageable.

We'll look at some particular techniques for constructively handling anger in the upcoming subchapter.

## DEVELOPING CALMING STRATEGIES: TAKING A BREAK AND COOLING DOWN

*"The quieter you become, the more you are able to hear."*
– Ram Dass

Have you ever had the feeling that your emotions are a train on fire, racing down the rails without any brakes? Anger in particular may feel so overwhelming and strong. However, you can learn to master your emotions, particularly anger, before they take you astray, just as a train requires a conductor to steer it.

Developing calming techniques is the main focus of this subchapter, which provides you with useful tools to take a break, relax, and control those strong emotions. It's about learning to become the conductor of your emotional train!

Let's consider a situation that is comparable. Consider yourself solving a difficult puzzle. You've been trying for a long time, but you're still having trouble fitting the final pieces. A sense of frustration begins to grow. Your muscles may tense, your face may become flushed, and you may even feel like throwing the puzzle across the room! All of them indicate that your level of rage is increasing. Your body seems to be telling you to take a break. You must relax." Learning to recognize these symptoms is the first step in creating calming practices.

Consider calming techniques to be your own anger management toolset. These are the methods you can employ to step back from the circumstance, calm your feelings, and regain composure. You may discover that certain soothing techniques are more effective for you than others, much like a toolbox contains various tools for various tasks. Finding what works best for "you" is the key. The following are some useful techniques for relaxation:

- **Inhaling deeply**: This is a timeless method of relaxation that works in practically any circumstance. Your heart rate can be lowered, your muscles relaxed, and your mind calmed by deep breathing. Try taking a slow, deep breath with your nose, holding it for a few seconds, and then letting it out through your mouth slowly. Imagine you're blowing up a balloon with each exhale.

A few minutes of mindfulness can help you de-stress and calm your mind.

- **Mindfulness**: Mindfulness is about focusing on the present moment without passing judgment, on your breath, your senses, or your thoughts without getting sucked into them.

- **Progressive Muscle Relaxation**: This technique involves tensing and relaxing various muscle groups in your body, starting from your toes and working your way up to your head. You tense each muscle group for a few seconds and then release it. This can help you relax and relieve physical tension.

- **Positive Self-Talk**: Your feelings can be greatly influenced by the things you tell yourself. Try using positive self-talk, like "I can handle this," to counter negative self-talk, like "I'm going to mess this up!" when you're upset. I'm doing my hardest."

- **Conceptualization**: Picture yourself in a serene location, such as a mountainside, a beach, or a forest. Shut your eyes and concentrate on this imagined location's sights, sounds, and scents. This might encourage relaxation and serve as a diversion from your rage.

- **Activity**: Physical: Exercise is a fantastic method to relieve stress and release stored energy. Take a bike ride, a jog, or a walk. Stretch, dance to your favorite music, or play a sport. Locate an activity that you enjoy and that helps you to feel calm and centered.

- **Creative Expression**: Take part in artistic endeavors that facilitate the healthy expression of your feelings. Sing, play music, write in a journal, paint, or draw. Anger and other challenging emotions can be effectively processed through creative expression.

- **Schedule a Rest**: Taking a break from the scenario that is causing you to feel upset is sometimes the best course of action. Find a peaceful location where you can gather your thoughts. Read a book, listen to music, or engage in another enjoyable activity.

Let's examine some actual instances of how children and teenagers might employ relaxing techniques:

Consider Emily, a student who is experiencing anxiety prior to a significant test. She could relax and concentrate on the task at hand by using deep breathing techniques. She might also talk to herself positively, telling herself that she has worked hard in her studies and that she can succeed.

Here's another illustration. Consider David, a teenager, who is upset following a fight with a friend. He may go away from the situation, take a stroll to decompress, and then speak with his friend when he's more composed.

Here's a fun exercise you can try: Make a "Calm Down Jar." Fill a jar with various calming activities that you can do when you're feeling stressed or angry, such as mindfulness exercises, deep breathing techniques, or positive affirmations. Choose an activity from the jar and try it whenever you're feeling overwhelmed. You can also make a "Relaxation Playlist." Make a list of songs that you find calming and relaxing, and listen to your relaxation playlist whenever you need to de-stress or cool down.

Recall that determining the most effective calming techniques is a personal process. What suits one individual may not suit another. It's crucial to try out many methods and determine which one "you" find most effective. You'll get better at controlling your anger and other challenging emotions the more you use these relaxing techniques. We'll look at healthy and productive ways to vent rage in the upcoming chapter.

## SELF-REFLECTION QUESTIONS

1.  What are some of the things that make you the angriest? Think about specific situations, people, or thoughts.

   _____

   _____

   _____

2. How do you usually express your anger? Is it through yelling, withdrawing, or something else?

_____

_____

_____

3. What are some of the physical signs you notice when you start to get angry (e.g., racing heart, clenched fists)?

_____

_____

_____

4. What are some things you can do to calm down when you feel your anger rising?

_____

_____

_____

5. How do you usually handle conflicts with others? Are there ways you could improve your communication skills?

_____

_____

_____

# TRANSFORMATIVE EXERCISES

1. Anger Triggers Chart: Create a chart with columns for "Situation,""Person,""Thought," and "Physical Signs." Over a week, track the times you feel angry and fill in the chart. This helps you identify patterns in your triggers.

2. "Cool-Down" Plan: Develop a personalized "cool-down" plan. List 3-5 specific calming strategies that work best for you (e.g., deep breathing, taking a walk, listening to music). Keep this list somewhere visible (like on your phone or in your locker) so you can refer to it when needed.

3. "I" Statement Practice: Practice using "I" statements to express your anger constructively. For example, instead of saying "You made me so mad!", say "I feel frustrated when..." This helps you communicate your feelings without blaming others.

4. Anger Thermometer: Draw a thermometer and label it from 1 (calm) to 10 (raging). When you start to feel angry, identify where you are on the thermometer. This helps you recognize when you need to use your calming strategies.

5. Role-Playing: Practice handling difficult conversations or conflicts through role-playing with a friend or family member. This allows you to try out different communication strategies in a safe environment.

# CHAPTER EIGHT

# BOOSTING YOUR SELF-ESTEEM:

# BELIEVING IN YOUR AWESOME

# SELF

---

*"Believe you can and you're halfway there."* – Theodore Roosevelt

Have you ever wished you had a superhero's abilities after seeing them? Wouldn't it be incredible to be able to fly, have superpowers, and be invisible? Guess what, though? Self-esteem is a superpower that you already possess that is even more potent than any of those. Like your own superpower, self-esteem gives you the courage to take on obstacles, have faith in yourself, and realize your goals.

Developing that superpower, believing in your amazing self, and realizing your full potential are the main topics of this chapter. Now is the moment to transform into your own superhero!

Let's consider a situation that is comparable. Consider yourself trying out for a school play or a sports team.

You're both anxious and thrilled. "What if I'm not good enough?" is one of the "what if" scenarios that begins to surface. "What if everyone laughs at me?" "What if I mess up?" These kinds of thinking indicate that you may need to improve your self-esteem.

The main component of self-esteem is your overall perception of oneself, or how you feel about yourself. It's about feeling good about yourself, appreciating your value, and having faith in your talents. You are more inclined to attempt new things, take chances, and overcome failures when your self-esteem is strong. Additionally, you're more likely to make wise decisions and maintain healthy relationships.

Conversely, poor self-esteem may make you more prone to self-doubt, shy away from difficulties, and give up easily. Additionally, you may be more susceptible to harmful influences like peer pressure or bullying.

It is not innate to have self-esteem. It evolves over time under the impact of your relationships, experiences, and the signals you receive from both yourself and other people. The good news is that you can develop and enhance your sense of self-worth. It gains strength with repeated use, just like a muscle.

**The following are essential elements of a good sense of self-worth:**

- Self-acceptance: Embracing your imperfections and being true to who you are. It's about accepting that flaws are a natural aspect of being human and that everyone makes mistakes.

- Self-confidence: Having faith in your own abilities and judgment. It's about having faith in your ability to manage any situation that arises.
- Self-respect: treating you with love and respect and valuing yourself. It all comes down to establishing sound boundaries and refusing to be mistreated by others.
- Sense of belonging: Having a sense of belonging and being a part of a community. It's about understanding that the people in your life appreciate and accept you.

**So, how do you increase your sense of self-worth? Here are a few effective tactics:**

- Tackle self-defeating thoughts: Be mindful of what you tell yourself. Are the majority of your thoughts constructive and upbeat, or are they critical of yourself and negative? If you catch yourself talking negatively to yourself, confront it. Consider whether this idea is accurate. Is there another perspective on the matter? Put more practical and upbeat ideas in place of pessimistic ones.

- Pay attention to your strengths: Everybody has their own abilities and strengths. Write down your accomplishments and good traits. Celebrate your accomplishments, no matter how minor, and concentrate on your strong points.

- Realistic goal-setting entails setting difficult but attainable objectives. Divide big objectives into smaller, easier-to-achieve steps. Every time you accomplish a goal, your self-esteem and confidence will grow.

- Be self-compassionate: Show yourself the same consideration and compassion that you would show a friend. Don't be too hard on yourself when you make a mistake. Take what you can from it and go forward.

- Be in the company of positive people: Spend time with people who give you confidence. Steer clear of those who are critical, nasty, or demeaning to you.

- Take good care of yourself by eating a balanced diet, getting adequate sleep, and exercising frequently. Your mental and emotional well-being can be significantly impacted by maintaining your physical health.

- Do what you enjoy: Take part in activities that make you happy and feel good. This could include everything from painting to listening to music to participating in sports.

Let's examine some actual instances of how children and teenagers might improve their sense of self: Consider Leo, a young child who is depressed over missing out on the baseball squad. He might tell himself that he did his best and that he became better during tryouts rather than that he is a failure. Additionally, he might remind himself of additional things he's good at, like drawing or playing the guitar.

Here's another illustration: Consider Maria, a teenager who is self-conscious about the way she looks. She could concentrate on her positive traits, such as her generosity and sense of humor, rather than evaluating herself against others. She could also remind oneself that everyone is unique and cultivate self-compassion.

Try this enjoyable hobby: "Self-Esteem Booster Jar." Assemble a jar with paper slips bearing affirmations such as "I am strong,""I am capable," or "I am loved." Take a slip of paper out of the jar and read it to yourself whenever you're feeling low.

Another exercise you could do is keeping a "Success Journal." Write down one successful thing you accomplished or something you're proud of every day. This might boost your confidence and help you concentrate on your good experiences.

Improving your self-esteem is a process rather than a final goal. It requires self-compassion, time, and work. However, the benefits are incalculable. You can achieve incredible things if you have faith in yourself. You'll have greater self-assurance, resilience, and a higher chance of realizing your goals.

We'll look at how to develop resilience and overcome setbacks in the upcoming chapter.

# IDENTIFYING YOUR STRENGTHS AND POSITIVE QUALITIES

*"Knowing yourself is the beginning of all wisdom."* –
Aristotle

Have you ever observed the variety of plants in a garden? Each one is lovely and special in its own way, whether they are small and delicate or tall and powerful. Similar to plants, each person has special traits and strengths that set them apart.

Discovering your inner garden, discovering your strengths, and appreciating the wonderful attributes that make you "you" are the main topics of this subchapter. You deserve to be honored for your excellence!

Let's consider a relatable example: Say you are working on a group project at school, and each person has different roles and responsibilities. Some people are good at research, while others are good at writing, and some are great at presenting. Each person contributes their own strengths to the project, making it stronger overall.

Just like that group project, you have your own set of positive qualities and strengths, which are the things you enjoy doing, the things you are good at, and the things that make you feel proud of yourself. Finding your strengths is like unearthing hidden gems within yourself; it can help you set reasonable goals, increase your self-confidence, and direct you toward pursuits and careers that are a good fit for you.

However, it might occasionally be challenging to recognize our own advantages. We may concentrate more on our shortcomings or areas of difficulty. It's crucial to take some time to think back on your experiences and pinpoint the traits that make you stand out because of this. **Here are a few examples of various strengths and admirable traits**:

- **Skills**: These are skills that come naturally to you. You may have talents in writing, painting, music, sports, or problem-solving.
- **Abilities**: These are skills that you have acquired and cultivated. You may be proficient in a foreign language, cooking, coding, or playing an instrument.

- **Personality traits are characteristics that characterize you**. You may be creative, resilient, kind, compassionate, or upbeat.

- **Values**: These are the things in life that you value most. Honesty, justice, friendship, or family may be important to you. So, how do you recognize your positive traits and strengths? Here are some useful strategies:

- **Think on your accomplishments**: What are you most proud of achieving? What obstacles have you surmounted? What compliments have you gotten from other people?

- **Consider your interests**: What kinds of things do you like to do? What do you have a strong interest in? Your strengths can frequently be found in your interests.

- **Get input**: Ask your loved ones, friends, instructors, or other responsible adults what they find admirable about you. Their viewpoints can provide insightful information about your advantages.

- **Take note of compliments**: Embrace accolades when they come your way! Don't minimize or dismiss it. Their praise can draw attention to your strong points.

- **Think about your values:** What do you consider important? What do you believe in? You can follow your ideals to find pursuits and activities that play to your talents.
- **Try something new**: You can uncover hidden abilities and strengths you were unaware you had by venturing outside of your comfort zone and attempting new things.

Let's examine some actual instances of how children and teenagers can recognize their strengths:

Consider Emily, a little child who enjoys lending a hand to others. She volunteers at a nearby animal shelter and is always there for her friends during difficult times. Kindness, sensitivity, and compassion may be among her strong points.

Here's another illustration: Consider David, a teenager with exceptional building skills. He always tinkers with projects in his garage because he loves doing manual labor. His strengths can include mechanical skills, problem-solving, and creativity.

Try this enjoyable hobby: Put together a "Strengths Collage." Collect periodicals, newspapers, and other sources, and then clip out pictures and phrases that best reflect your good traits and strong points. Make a collage that highlights all of your wonderful qualities.

One more thing you may do is to make a "Strengths Inventory." Make a list of your many positive traits and strengths (you can find lists online if you need inspiration). Go over the list and marks off the attributes you believe best define you. Then jot down particular instances where you have exhibited those traits.

A vital first step in developing self-confidence and self-esteem is recognizing your good attributes and strengths. It enables you to value yourself, value your individuality, and concentrate on your strengths. It's about honoring the lovely plants that make you "you" and your inner garden.

How to leverage your strengths to develop objectives and realize your ambitions will be covered in the upcoming section.

# CHALLENGING NEGATIVE SELF-TALK:

# REPLACING PUT-DOWNS WITH

# ENCOURAGEMENT

*"Watch your thoughts, they become words. Watch your words, they become actions. Watch your actions, they become habits. Watch your habits, they become character. Watch your character, it becomes your destiny."* – Lao Tzu

This subchapter is all about learning to tame that inner critic and replace negative self-talk with positive encouragement. Imagine that you have a little voice inside your head that is constantly chattering away.

Your inner voice can be critical and negative, like a bully putting you down, or it can be supportive and encouraging, like a cheerleader encouraging you on. This inner voice is your self-talk, and it can have a huge impact on how you feel about yourself and what you can achieve.

Let's consider a situation that is comparable. Consider yourself a candidate for the school play. You're both anxious and thrilled. "What if I forget my lines?" is the question that begins to nag at the back of your mind.

- "What if everyone laughs at me?"
- "What if I'm not good enough?"

These are instances of negative self-talk, or the disparaging remarks we say to ourselves that can cause us to feel anxious and unconfident.

- There are numerous ways that negative self-talk manifests itself. It could be pessimistic ("I'll never be able to do this."), critical ("I'm so stupid!"), or judgmental ("I'm such a klutz!").

- Additionally, it may entail highlighting your shortcomings ("I'm just not good at anything." or exaggerating your errors, "I always mess everything up!").

Your self-esteem can be severely harmed by negative self-talk. When things go hard, it might make you feel bad about yourself, less willing to take chances, and more ready to give up. It's like to having a tiny gremlin in your head that is always attempting to ruin your achievement.

The good news is that you can stop talking negatively to yourself. You have the ability to confront those pessimistic ideas and swap them out for more uplifting and supportive ones. It's similar to teaching that inner gremlin to stop being a bully and start cheering.

**The following techniques will help you combat negative self-talk:**

- Be conscious of your mind: Being aware of what you're telling yourself is the first step. When those negative thoughts arise, pay attention to them. Make an effort to pinpoint the precise circumstances or triggers that appear to cause them.

- Challenge the veracity of your thoughts: Consider whether this thought is accurate. What are the arguments in favor of and against it? When we closely examine our negative beliefs, we frequently discover that they are founded on assumptions or fears rather than facts.

- Reframe pessimistic thoughts: Aim to adopt a new perspective on the matter. Is there a more optimistic or well-rounded way to look at it? For example, instead of thinking "I'm going to fail this test," you could think "I've studied hard, and I'm going to do my best. I can still gain knowledge even if I don't receive the grade I desire.

- Substitute positive affirmations for negative thoughts: Replace a negative thinking with a positive affirmation after you've contested it. These are self-affirming phrases that you can say to yourself on a daily basis. For instance, you could tell yourself, "I am capable and I believe in myself," as opposed to, "I am not good enough."

- Practice self-compassion by treating yourself with the same consideration and kindness that you would show a friend. Don't be too hard on yourself when you make a mistake. Take what you can from it and go forward.

Let's examine some actual instances of how children and teenagers can combat self-defeating thoughts:

Consider Alex, a young child who is anxious about trying out for the school's soccer squad. He may say to himself, "I'm not good enough." Everyone will laugh at me when I make a mistake.

By asking himself, "Is it really true that I'm not good enough?," he could confront those beliefs. I've been honing my skills through a lot of practice. Furthermore, it won't be catastrophic if I don't make the squad.

I can still enjoy playing soccer. An example of a positive affirmation he may use to counter those negative ideas would be, "I am a skilled soccer player, and I am confident in my abilities."

Here's another illustration: Consider a depressed adolescent named Sarah who was not invited to a party. She may be saying to herself, "No one likes me." It's usually me who is excluded.

By asking herself, "Is it true that no one likes me?," she could confront those beliefs. Other pals are concerned about me. Perhaps there's a reason why I wasn't invited to this specific gathering. It does not imply that I am disliked by anyone.

Positive statements like "I am a valuable friend, and I am surrounded by people who love and appreciate me" might then take the place of such pessimistic beliefs.

Try this entertaining exercise: Make a "Negative Thought Catcher." Draw a picture of a net or trap and decorate it. Then, whenever you see a negative thought, picture yourself catching it in your net. Write down the negative thought and question its veracity. Finally, write down a positive affirmation to replace it.

Another activity is to make a "Positive Self-Talk Journal." Every day, record any negative thoughts you've had and how you overcame them. You can also record any positive affirmations you used to replace those negative thoughts.

This will allow you to monitor your progress and see how your self-talk is evolving.

One of the most effective strategies for enhancing resilience and self-worth is learning to confront negative self-talk. It supports you in appreciating your abilities, realizing your worth, and having faith in your capacity to succeed. It's about supporting oneself at every turn and turning into your own best friend.

We'll look at how to leverage your strengths to develop objectives and realize your desires in the upcoming chapter.

## SELF-REFLECTION QUESTIONS

1. What are some things you do well or enjoy doing?

   _____

   _____

   _____

2. What are some qualities you like about yourself (e.g., kindness, humor, creativity)?

   _____

   _____

   _____

3. What are some negative thoughts you sometimes have about yourself?

_____

_____

_____

4. How do these negative thoughts make you feel?

_____

_____

_____

5. What are some small steps you could take to start building your self-esteem?

_____

_____

_____

## TRANSFORMATIVE EXERCISES

1. "I Am Awesome" List: Create a list of at least 10 things you like about yourself. These can be talents, skills, personality traits, or anything else that makes you feel good about whom you are. Review this list regularly.

2. Strength Spotting: Ask three people you trust (friends, family, and teachers) to tell you what they think your strengths are. Compare their answers to your own list and see if you notice any patterns.

3. Challenge Negative Self-Talk: When you notice a negative thought, ask yourself: Is this thought

really true? What's the evidence for and against it? Is there another way to look at the situation? Replace the negative thought with a more positive and realistic one.

4. Goal Setting with Strengths: Choose a small, achievable goal that you can work towards. Think about how your strengths can help you reach that goal. Celebrate your progress along the way.

5. Acts of Kindness: Do something kind for someone else, whether it's helping a friend, volunteering in your community, or simply offering a compliment. Helping others can boost your own self-esteem.

# CHAPTER NINE

# BUILDING RESILIENCE:

# BOUNCING BACK FROM

# CHALLENGES

---

*"The oak fought the wind and was broken, the willow bent when it must and survived."* – Robert Jordan

There are ups and downs in life. Sometimes everything goes without a hitch, and other times we encounter difficulties, disappointments, and setbacks. It's simply a characteristic of humanity. However, resilience—the capacity to overcome hardship, grow from our experiences, and continue on even when things get difficult—is what distinguishes those who succeed from those who struggle.

Building resilience, cultivating inner strength, and learning to weather life's storms with more ease and confidence are the main topics of this chapter. Now is the moment to become a rock of resilience!

Let's consider a situation that is comparable. Consider yourself engaged in a project that holds great significance for you. Even if you've invested a great deal of time and energy, things don't work out. Perhaps you encounter unforeseen challenges, receive a poor grade, or have your project rejected. What would you do? Would you become disheartened and quit? Or would you get back up, take what you've learned, and try again?

Your resilience is demonstrated by how you handle difficulties. Even those who are resilient can have setbacks. Like everyone else, they encounter setbacks and challenges. However, they are able to handle stress, adjust to change, and overcome hardship. They view obstacles as opportunities for growth and learning.

Being resilient is not a fixed quality. It's a skill that may be improved and reinforced. It's similar to developing a muscle in that it gets stronger with use.

**The following are some essential elements of resilience**:

- The ability to see the bright side of life and have faith that things will improve in due time is known as optimism. Even in challenging circumstances, optimists have a propensity to see the positive.

- Acceptance: Recognizing and embracing the things that are beyond your control. It's about focusing on the things that you "can" influence while acknowledging that some things are out of your control.

- Perspective: Maintaining perspective and avoiding exaggerating minor issues. It's about knowing that setbacks are fleeting and that they don't define you.
- Having a network of people who are there to assist and encourage you is known as a support system. It's about understanding that you have people that care about you and that you're not alone.
- Taking care of your physical and mental health is known as self-care. It all comes down to eating well, exercising frequently, getting adequate sleep, and doing things you enjoy.
- Problem-solving abilities: Possessing the capacity to recognize issues, generate potential fixes, and act upon them. When faced with obstacles, it's about being proactive and resourceful.
- Meaning and purpose: Having a feeling of purpose and meaning in life. It's about finding meaning in your experiences and relating to something greater than yourself.

**So, how might resilience is developed? Here are a few effective tactics**:

- Challenge pessimistic thoughts: Be mindful of your thoughts and confront any self-critical or pessimistic thought patterns. Put more practical and upbeat ideas in place of pessimistic ones.

- Pay attention to your strengths: Recognize your abilities and strengths and figure out how to use them to your everyday life. You may overcome obstacles and increase your confidence by concentrating on your strengths.

- Take note of your errors: Consider errors as chances for development and learning. Don't focus on your shortcomings. Rather, ask yourself: What can I take out from this? What can I do differently the next time?

- Create a network of support by connecting with individuals you can trust and who care about you. Discuss your difficulties with them, and don't be scared to seek assistance.

- Take care of yourself: Put your mental and physical health first. Eat well, exercise frequently, get adequate sleep, and partake in enjoyable hobbies.

- Build your ability to solve problems: Develop your ability to see issues, come up with answers, and act. Divide complex issues into smaller, easier-to-manage phases.

- Find meaning and purpose: Whether it's volunteering, following a passion, or interacting with your community, find a connection with something greater than yourself.

Let's examine some actual instances of how children and teenagers might develop resilience: Consider a little girl named Maya who is depressed at not being selected for the school's dancing squad. She could work on honing her dancing abilities and try out again the following year rather than giving up on her dream. She might also find other ways to exhibit her passion of dance, like taking a dance class.

Here's another illustration: Consider David, a teenager who is having trouble in a challenging class. He might ask a tutor or his teacher for assistance rather than giving up. In order to learn the content, he may potentially organize a study club with his peers.

Try this enjoyable hobby: Put together a "Resilience Toolkit." Put things in a box that serve as a reminder of your coping mechanisms, support network, and strengths. This could include pictures of your loved ones, motivational sayings, or little items that symbolize your interests and pastimes. Open your Resilience Toolkit if you're having a hard time to get some support and encouragement.

An additional task that you could attempt is crafting a "Resilience Story." Consider a moment when you had to overcome a challenging situation. Jot down the specifics of the circumstance, the actions you did to resolve it, and the lessons you drew away from it. You can increase your confidence and fortitude for upcoming difficulties by thinking back on your prior achievements.

Developing resilience takes a lifetime. It requires self-compassion, time, and work. However, the benefits are incalculable. Resilient people are better able to deal with life's ups and downs, grow from their experiences, and realize their full potential. We'll look at ways to connect with people and create healthy connections in the upcoming chapter.

## UNDERSTANDING RESILIENCE: WHAT MAKES YOU STRONG?

*"Resilience is not about going through life unscathed. It's about finding the strength to rise again, no matter how many times you fall."* – Unknown

Life can be unpredictable. Sometimes you hit a home run, and other times you strike out. The manner you respond to curveballs when they occur is more important than "avoiding" them. Resilience is useful in this situation. It is the inner power that enables you to overcome obstacles, grow from your errors, and continue on your path even when times are difficult.

This subchapter focuses on defining resilience, examining the elements that influence it, and realizing the incredible ability you already possess to handle whatever challenge life presents.

Think of yourself like a tree in a forest. Tall and sturdy, some trees can withstand any storm. Others are more delicate and can be broken by powerful winds.

Being resilient is similar to having strong roots that support you and enable you to withstand life's ups and downs. Being flexible and resourceful is more important than being unbeatable.

Consider a moment when you encountered a difficulty. Perhaps you received a poor grade on an exam, had a falling out with a friend, or were not selected for the team you tried out for. What was your reaction? Were you defeated and gave up? Did you get back up and try again? You can tell how resilient you are by how you handled that issue.

The ability to be resilient is not innate. It's a skill that you acquire over time, just like learning to play an instrument or ride a bike. It can also be improved with practice, just like any other ability. **Resilience is composed of the following essential components:**

- Positivity: recognizing the positive aspects of circumstances, even in the face of adversity. It's about having optimism for the future and having faith in your capacity to overcome obstacles. It's important to balance the bad with optimism rather than to ignore it.

- Sturdy Relationships: Having a network of individuals who are there for you when you need support and encouragement. These could be mentors, coaches, instructors, friends, or relatives. When you're going through a tough moment, knowing that you have people who care about you can make all the difference.

- Self-Awareness: Awareness of your own feelings, strengths, and shortcomings. It's about understanding your stressors, your coping mechanisms, and how you respond to obstacles. Being self-aware enables you to consciously choose how you react in trying circumstances. The ability to control your emotions and impulses is known as self-regulation. It's about finding healthy ways to express your emotions and avoiding having them control you. Self-regulation enables you to maintain composure and concentration in the face of stress or agitation.

- Problem-Solving Skills: The capacity to recognize issues generate ideas for fixes, and act on them. It's about overcoming barriers with ingenuity and resourcefulness. Instead of becoming bogged down in the issue, problem-solving abilities enable you to move forward and discover answers.

- Context and Goal: possessing a feeling of direction and significance in life. It's about finding meaning in your experiences and relating to something greater than yourself. You may conquer obstacles with courage and determination if you have a sense of purpose.

Let's examine some actual instances of how these components support resilience: Consider Maria, a young girl trying out for the school play. Although she doesn't play the protagonist, she does play a supporting role. Her feeling disappointed but then concentrating on the bright side—she's still in the show, she'll have experience, and she can put in a lot of effort to get better for next auditions—would be a resilient reaction. This demonstrates self-control and a good outlook.

Here's another illustration: Consider David, a teenager who is having trouble in a challenging class. He might divide the subject down into smaller, more digestible portions, organize a study group with classmates, or ask his teacher for further help if he feels overwhelmed and decides to give up. This illustrates the use of a support network and problem-solving abilities.

Try this enjoyable hobby. Make your own "Resilience Recipe." Consider the components of resilience we covered and how you may use them. Jot down particular instances from your life that illustrate each component. This might assist you in identifying areas for improvement as well as your current strengths.

Another thing you might try is to interview someone you respect who has overcome problems in their life. Ask them about what helped them to be resilient. What lessons did their experiences teach them? What guidance would they offer to someone going through a challenging moment? Gaining knowledge from the experiences of others may be tremendously motivating and encouraging.

One of the most important steps in developing resilience is realizing your strengths. It's about identifying the resources you currently possess and learning how to make the most of them.

# DEVELOPING COPING SKILLS:

# STRATEGIES FOR DEALING WITH

# STRESS

*"Stress is not what happens to us. It's our reaction to what happens to us, and our reaction is something we can control."* – Hans Selye

Sometimes it seems like life is moving too quickly. Activities, friends, family, and school can all become too much to handle. We refer to the sensation of being overpowered as stress. Stress is a natural part of life, how we respond to it can have a significant impact.

The focus of this subchapter is on coping skills development, or how to manage stress in a healthy way so that you may remain resilient, balanced, and prepared to face any challenge. It's similar to creating your own customized stress-reduction equipment!

Let's consider a situation that is comparable. Imagine that a significant test is approaching. You've put a lot of effort into your studies, but your anxiety persists. You may feel agitated, lose your appetite, or have problems falling asleep. All of them indicate that you're under stress.

Stress is how your body responds to pressures or difficulties. It warns you of any issues like an integrated alarm system. In fact, a small amount of stress can be beneficial, inspiring you to work harder in your studies or perform better. However, stress can negatively impact both your physical and mental well-being if it persists or becomes too much to handle.

Coping skills are the methods you employ to deal with stress. They are the instruments in your arsenal for relieving stress. Certain coping mechanisms are more beneficial than others. Exercise, for instance, is a healthy coping mechanism, but numbing your emotions with drugs or alcohol is not.

**The following list of coping ability categories includes examples**:

- Problems -Focused Coping: The goal of these tactics is to deal with the stressor directly. Examples include making a study plan for the test, discussing your worries with your teacher, and breaking down a big assignment into manageable chunks.

- Emotion-Focused Coping: These techniques are meant to help you deal with the emotions that arise from stress. Some of these techniques include deep breathing exercises, mindfulness meditation, music, spending time in nature, and talking to friends or family.

- Avoidance Coping (Unhealthy): Avoidance coping involves avoiding or running away from the stressful situation, which may offer short-term respite but isn't a healthy long-term solution. Examples include putting off studying for the test, acting as though the test isn't happening, and isolating oneself from friends and family.

It's important to have a range of coping techniques so that you have different options depending on the situation.

**You can use the following specific coping mechanisms**:

- **Breathing deeply**: Your pulse rate can be lowered, your muscles relaxed, and your thoughts calmed by deep breathing. Try taking a slow, deep breath with your nose, holding it for a few seconds, and then letting it out through your mouth slowly.

- **Meditation with Mindfulness**: The goal of mindfulness is to focus on the here and now without passing judgment. It can assist you in becoming more conscious of your feelings and ideas without allowing them to consume you. Numerous guided mindfulness meditations are accessible via applications or the internet.

- **Muscle Relaxation Progressively**: This method entails tensing and relaxing various body muscle groups. It might assist to alleviate bodily tension and induce relaxation.

- **Physical Activity**: Exercise is a fantastic method to relieve tension and release stored-up energy. Whether it's swimming, dancing, running, or sports, choose something you love to do.

- **Creative Expression**: Take part in artistic endeavors that facilitate emotional expression. Anything from writing and playing music to painting and drawing could fall under this category.

- **Time Spent in Nature**: It has been demonstrated that spending time in nature lowers stress and elevates mood. Take a stroll in the park, go hiking in the forest, or just relax outside and breathe in the fresh air.

- **Speaking with a Trusted Person**: You can get perspective and process your stress by talking to a friend, family member, or therapist about how you're feeling.

- **Getting Adequate Sleep**: Lack of sleep can exacerbate stress. Try to get 8 to 10 hours per night.

- **Maintaining a Healthful Diet**: Consuming wholesome foods can help you feel happier and have more energy. Steer clear of sugary drinks and excessive caffeine as these might exacerbate anxiety.

Let's examine some actual instances of how children and teenagers can apply coping mechanisms:

Consider Alex, a student who feels overburdened by his coursework. By making a study plan and dividing his responsibilities into smaller, more doable tasks, he could employ problem-focused coping. He could also employ emotion-focused coping by taking walks or music breaks.

Here's another illustration: Consider a teenager named Sarah who is experiencing anxiety due to a social circumstance. She could use positive self-talk to increase her confidence and mindfulness meditation to soothe her anxiety.

Try this enjoyable hobby: Put together a "Coping Skills Toolbox." Stuff a box with objects that symbolize various coping mechanisms. This could be a list of guided meditations, a journal for recording your thoughts and feelings, a coloring book for creative expression, or a stress ball for squeezing. Reach for a coping mechanism from your toolbox whenever you're feeling anxious.

Another exercise you can try is making a "Stress Thermometer." Draw a thermometer and label it from 1 (low stress) to 10 (high stress). Throughout the day, check in with yourself and rate your stress level. This will help you become more aware of your stress triggers and use your coping skills proactively.

Coping skills development is a crucial component of resilience and stress management; it involves learning to identify your stress triggers, comprehending your emotional reactions, and creating healthy strategies for overcoming obstacles.

By assembling your stress-busting toolkit, you'll be better prepared to handle life's ups and downs and to thrive even under pressure. In the following chapter, we'll look at how to connect with others and build healthy relationships.

## SELF-REFLECTION QUESTIONS

1. Think about a time you faced a challenge or setback. How did you react?

   _____

   _____

   _____

2. What are some things that help you to cope with stress or difficult emotions?

   _____

   _____

   _____

3. Who are the people in your life you can turn to for support?

   _____

   _____

   _____

4. What are some things you do to take care of your physical and mental health?

   _____

   _____

   _____

5. What are some areas where you'd like to build more resilience?

_____

_____

_____

## TRANSFORMATIVE EXERCISES

1. "Resilience Recipe": Think about the key components of resilience (optimism, acceptance, perspective, support, self-care, problem-solving, meaning). Write down specific examples of how you demonstrate each of these in your life. This helps you recognize your existing strengths.

2. Stress-Busting Toolkit: Create a list of 5-10 coping strategies that work well for you. These could be deep breathing, exercise, listening to music, talking to a friend, etc. Keep this list handy so you can refer to it when needed.

3. "Challenge-Response-Growth" Journal: When you face a challenge, write about it in a journal. Describe the challenge, how you responded, and what you learned from the experience. Focus on the growth you experienced as a result of the challenge.

4. Support System Map: Draw a map of your support system. Include family, friends, teachers, coaches, or anyone else you can rely on. Think about how each person provides support and how you can strengthen those connections.

5. Self-Care Schedule: Create a weekly schedule that includes specific times for self-care activities. This could be anything from getting enough sleep and eating healthy meals to engaging in hobbies and spending time in nature. Prioritize these activities just as you would any other important appointment

# CHAPTER TEN

# PROBLEM-SOLVING

# SUPERPOWERS: TACKLING

# CHALLENGES LIKE A PRO

---

*"Obstacles are those frightful things you see when you take your eyes off your goal."* – Henry Ford

There are many mysteries in life. Certain problems, like deciding what to wear in the morning, are simple to resolve. Others, such as handling a disagreement with a buddy or taking on a challenging school assignment, are more complicated. We call these puzzles—no matter how big or small—problems. You need tactics to deal with issues in the same way that a detective requires instruments to unravel a mystery.

This chapter is all about giving you superpowers to solve problems and make you an expert at overcoming obstacles and coming up with workable answers. Let your inner problem-solver loose!

Let's look at a situation that is relatable. Imagine you've been working really hard on a science project, and the day before it's due, your computer crashes, and you lose all your work. Panic sets in. What are you doing? Do you cry and give up? Is your computer to blame? Or do you inhale deeply and attempt to think of a solution? Your ability to solve problems will determine how you respond to this circumstance.

The process of recognizing an issue, investigating potential fixes, selecting the best course of action, and implementing it is known as problem-solving. It's an essential ability for overcoming obstacles and accomplishing your objectives in life.

**Here's a methodical approach to solving problems effectively:**

1.  **Define the issue**: Describe the specific difficulty you are encountering. Give specifics. Rather than stating "I have a problem with school," attempt "I'm struggling to understand the material in my math class."

2.  **Look into potential fixes**: Come up with as many ideas as you can, even if they initially appear absurd or unfeasible. At this point, don't evaluate your ideas. Creating a large number of possibilities is the aim. For the arithmetic challenge, for instance, some solutions include speaking with the teacher, asking a friend for assistance, looking up resources online, or joining a study group.

3. **Assess the solutions**: Take into account the advantages and disadvantages of every option. Which choices are the most practical and likely to work? Which of these could have adverse effects? Speaking with the teacher about the arithmetic example is perhaps a better course of action than ignoring the issue completely.

4. **Select the optimal option**: Choose the option you believe has the best chance of succeeding based on your assessment. Think about your capabilities, your resources, and the possible consequences of your decision.

5. **Develop a strategy**: How are you going to carry out your selected course of action? Divide the steps into more manageable, smaller tasks. For the math problem, the plan can be: "
    1. Talk to the teacher after class tomorrow.
    2. Ask Sarah for help with the homework.
    3. Search for videos explaining the concepts online."

6. **Action**: Implement your strategy. Don't put things off or offer excuses. You'll find a solution sooner if you get started.

7. **Assess the outcomes**: Was your solution successful? If so, fantastic! Otherwise, don't give up. Take what you've learned from it and attempt something new. Perhaps the teacher recommended a different resource, or perhaps the web videos were more beneficial than Sarah's explanation.

Let's look at some real-life examples of how kids and teens can use these problem-solving steps:

Consider Alex, a child who is being harassed at school. He was able to pinpoint the issue as "Jake is bullying me." He could look into options including talking to a responsible adult, learning self-defense skills, avoiding Jake, or attempting to speak with Jake directly. He may decide to speak with a trusted adult and acquire aggressive communication techniques after weighing his options.

Here's another illustration: Consider Sarah, a teenager who has trouble managing her time. One way she could describe the issue is "I'm always feeling overwhelmed and stressed because I have too much to do."

She might look into options like making a timetable, setting priorities, assigning duties, or learning to say "no" to excessive commitments. She can decide to make a weekly timetable and set priorities for her duties, starting with the most crucial ones.

Try this enjoyable hobby: A "Problem-Solving Flowchart." should be made. Create a flowchart with boxes for each stage of the problem-solving procedure (problem identification, solution exploration, etc.). Walk through the flowchart, recording your ideas and actions at each stage, using a real-world problem or a fictional one.

"What Would You Do?" is another game you might try? Create a variety of difficult situations and talk about how you would resolve them. You can use this to engage in enjoyable problem-solving activity.

Keep in mind that addressing problems is a skill that requires practice. Your ability to overcome obstacles will improve as you apply these strategies more frequently. It's about gaining the self-assurance and abilities to confront issues head-on, not about completely avoiding them.

You'll be able to handle life's curveballs more easily and accomplish your objectives with more assurance if you master problem-solving. We'll look at how to connect with others for support and create wholesome connections in the following chapter.

# THE PROBLEM-SOLVING STEPS: A

## STEP-BY-STEP GUIDE

*"Every problem is a gift—without problems we would not grow."* – Steve Chandler

Consider yourself a chef attempting to prepare the ideal meal. You wouldn't just haphazardly combine materials, would you? To guarantee a wonderful result, you would follow a recipe exactly. Similar to a recipe, problem-solving is a process with distinct steps that can help you arrive at a workable answer.

This subchapter provides you with a step-by-step manual for addressing problems effectively and transforming obstacles into chances for development and education. Put on your chef's hat and come up with some answers now!

Let's look at a situation that is relatable. Let's say you are looking forward to a school field trip but lack the funds to make it happen. This is the "problem ingredient." You want to travel, but something is stopping you. How does one "cook up" a solution now?

**The steps to follow in the problem-solving process are your recipe:**

i. Step 1: Determine the Issue (Name the Dish): Clearly state the issue. What is the challenge, exactly? Give specifics. It will be easier to discover a solution if you are more specific about the issue. For example, instead of saying "I have a problem," say "I don't have enough money for the field trip."

ii.     Step 2: Gather Your Ingredients and Investigate Potential Solutions: Come up with as many ideas as you can. At this point, use your imagination and don't rule out any ideas, even if they appear absurd or unrealistic. Creating a vast array of possibilities is the aim. Solutions for the field trip example include asking my parents for a payment advance on my allowance, working more hours to generate money, asking a family member for a loan, setting up a fundraiser, and discussing payment choices with the teacher.

iii.     Step 3: Assess the Solutions by Tasting Your Choices: Examine each solution's benefits and drawbacks carefully. Which choices are practical, realistic, and likely to work? Which of these could have adverse effects? Asking for an advance on the allowance for the field trip might be possible, but with the short notice, planning a large fundraising event might be more difficult.

iv.     Step 4: Pick Your Recipe or the Best Solution: Choose the option you believe has the best chance of succeeding based on your assessment. Think about your capabilities, your resources, and the possible consequences of your decision. Perhaps the best course of action is to discuss payment arrangements with the teacher.

v.   Step 5: Make a Strategy (Get Your Ingredients Ready): How are you going to put your selected solution into practice? Divide the steps into more manageable, smaller jobs. One possible plan for the field trip is:

1. Discuss payment arrangements with the teacher after class tomorrow.
2. Inquire with my parents whether I can work extra hours to supplement my income.
3. Find out whether any financial help or scholarships are offered for field excursions.

Step 6: Act (Get the Cooking Started!): Implement your strategy. Don't put things off or offer excuses. You'll find a solution sooner if you get started. Go speak with the instructor, inquire about duties, and look into scholarships.

Step 7: Assess Outcomes (Taste): Did your remedy make a difference? If so, fantastic! Otherwise, don't give up. Take what you've learned from it and attempt something new. Although they recommended a fundraising concept, the teacher may not have offered payment arrangements. Be adaptable and ready to change your strategy.

Let's examine some other real-world instances where children and teenagers can apply these problem-solving techniques:

Consider Alex, a student who finds it difficult to stay on top of his assignments. Identifying the problem, he states, "I'm always falling behind on my assignments." He considers the following options: make a study plan, get tutoring, discuss extensions with his teacher, and cut back on extracurricular activities. He assesses and decides that making a study plan and speaking with his teacher is the best course of action.

He devises a strategy:

1. Make a weekly timetable.
2. Discuss with the instructor which assignments are most crucial.
3. The schedule helps, but talking to the teacher was the most helpful part!" he says after acting.

Here's another illustration: Consider a teenage girl named Sarah and her best friend at odds. The issue, as she puts it, is that "my best friend and I are not talking to each other." Giving her friend space, writing her a letter, speaking with her face-to-face, or asking a common acquaintance to mediate are some of the possibilities she considers.

She weighs her options and decides that speaking with her friend face-to-face is the best course of action. She intends to:

1. Invite her to coffee with me.

2. Use 'I' expressions to express my feelings to her.

3. Talking in person helped a lot, we were able to understand each other better," she says after acting.

Try this enjoyable hobby: Construct a "Problem-Solving Wheel." Divide a circle into seven parts, each of which represents a phase in the problem-solving process. Spin the wheel and land on a step when you're having trouble. Before going on to the next stage, concentrate on that one and finish it.

You might also try playing "Problem-Solving Pictionary." The other person must vocally go through the seven steps of problem-solving after one person illustrates a difficult scenario in order to come up with a solution.

Keep in mind that addressing problems is a skill that requires practice. Your ability to overcome obstacles will improve as you apply these strategies more frequently. It's about gaining the self-assurance and abilities to confront issues head-on, not about completely avoiding them.

You'll be able to accomplish your goals with more assurance and handle life's curveballs more easily if you can master these steps.

## BRAINSTORMING SOLUTIONS:

## THINKING OUTSIDE THE BOX

*"The best way to have a good idea is to have a lot of ideas."* – Linus Pauling

Consider yourself an inventor attempting to develop a novel device. You would not simply halt at the first thought that occurs to you, would you? You would push the limits of what is feasible, experiment with different designs, and investigate other possibilities. That is precisely what brainstorming is all about: coming up with a ton of ideas, even the ones that appear ridiculous, to solve an issue. This section serves as your manual for developing your creative problem-solving skills, thinking creatively, and brainstorming techniques. Now is the time to let your inner innovator go!

Let's consider a situation that is comparable. Consider organizing a friend's surprise birthday celebration. You're not sure where to begin, but you want it to be unique and unforgettable. You need ideas for everything, including the theme, the setting, and the activities! Here's when brainstorming is useful.

This method of coming up with a lot of ideas quickly is called brainstorming. It's about using your imagination, investigating other options, and not passing judgment on your ideas too quickly. The objective is to generate a variety of possibilities, including those that appear absurd or unfeasible. A "crazy" concept could lead to a very wonderful solution—you never know.

**The following are some essential guidelines for productive brainstorming:**

- **Quantity is more important than quality**. The objective is to come up with as many ideas as you can, regardless of how ridiculous or absurd they may appear. Don't think about how "good" or "bad" an idea is at this point. Finding a brilliant idea is more likely the more ideas you have.

- **No opinion**: When brainstorming, avoid evaluating or criticizing ideas. Any and all suggestions are appreciated. Making snap decisions can hinder your creativity and keep you from considering every option.

- **Expand on each other's concepts**: Draw inspiration from others' ideas to develop your own.

Ideas can be combined, altered, or used as a basis for whole new concepts.

- **Be visual**: Write down your thoughts on a sheet of paper, a flip chart, or even a whiteboard. You can think more creatively if you visualize your ideas. You can use the following brainstorming methods:

- **Understanding**: For a few minutes, set a timer, and without bothering about grammar or spelling, jot down everything that comes to mind concerning the situation. Simply let your mind to wander.

- **Mind mapping**: Place the problem in the middle of the paper and then create branches that represent various problem categories or facets. Next, generate concepts associated with every category.

- **SCAMPER**: Substitute, Combine, Adapt, Modify/Magnify/Minimize, Put to new purposes, Eliminate, and Reverse are the words that this acronym represents. Think about how you can enhance or change preexisting concepts by using these prompts.

- **Acting out roles**: Ask yourself how someone else—a buddy, a superhero, or a famous person—would handle the situation.

- **"What If" Questions**: To consider several options, ask yourself "what if" questions. "What if we had unlimited resources?" is one example. "What if we could travel through time?"

Return to the example of the surprise birthday celebration. By employing brainstorming techniques, you may generate concepts such as: Superhero parties, Hollywood parties, tropical luaus, escape room challenges, and backyard camping adventures are some examples of the themes.

A park, community center, someone's home, rented event venue, or a boat excursion are some examples of the locations. Activities include games, a scavenger hunt, a DIY photo booth, a surprise video montage, a dance party, and karaoke.

When you start organizing the party, you'll have a ton of possibilities to pick from if you brainstorm a variety of ideas.

Let's examine some further actual instances of how children and teenagers might apply brainstorming:

Consider Alex, a student who is attempting to think of a research paper topic. He might create a list of possible subjects using free-writing, then select the most intriguing and pertinent ones.

Here's another illustration: Consider Sarah, a teenager, attempting to resolve a dispute with her buddy. She may utilize role-playing to understand her friend's point of view and devise solutions that meet their needs.

Try this enjoyable hobby: Pick an issue, real or imagined, and come up with as many answers as you can using various brainstorming approaches. Remember to put all of your thoughts on paper, regardless of how absurd they may seem.

Organizing a "brainstorming party" with friends or family is an additional activity you might attempt. Select an issue and collaborate to find solutions. Your chances of coming up with more ideas increase with the number of participants.

Always keep in mind that brainstorming is a skill that requires practice. Your ability to think creatively and come up with original solutions will improve with practice.

It's about embracing your creativity, letting go of your inhibitions, and considering every option. Gaining proficiency in brainstorming techniques will enable you to approach any problem with assurance and originality.

## SELF-REFLECTION QUESTIONS

1. Think about a recent problem you solved. What steps did you take?

   _____

   _____

   _____

2. What are some of your go-to strategies for dealing with challenges?

   _____

   _____

   _____

3. Do you tend to jump to solutions quickly, or do you take time to explore different options?

   _____

   _____

   _____

4. What are some common obstacles that prevent you from solving problems effectively?

   _____

   _____

   _____

5. What could you do to improve your problem-solving skills?

_____

_____

_____

## TRANSFORMATIVE EXERCISES

1. Problem-Solving Flowchart: Create a visual flowchart outlining the steps of the problem-solving process (identify, explore, evaluate, choose, plan, act, evaluate). Use it to guide you through a recent or hypothetical problem.

2. "What Would You Do?" Scenarios: Come up with different challenging scenarios (e.g., conflict with a friend, difficult school assignment, feeling overwhelmed). Practice walking through the problem-solving steps to find solutions. Do this with a friend or family member for added fun and perspective.

3. Brainstorming Challenge: Choose a problem and set a timer for 5 minutes. Try to generate as many solutions as possible within that time, without judging the ideas. Focus on quantity over quality.

4. "Pros and Cons" Chart: When evaluating solutions, create a T-chart. List the pros (advantages) of each solution on one side and the

cons (disadvantages) on the other. This can help you make more informed decisions.

5. "Problem-Solver's Journal": Keep a journal where you document the problems you face, the solutions you try, and the results. Reflect on what worked well and what you could do differently next time. This helps you track your progress and learn from your experiences.

# CHAPTER ELEVEN

# KEEPING IT UP: MAKING CBT A

# PART OF YOUR LIFE

---

*"The mind is everything. What you think you become."* –
Buddha

From identifying thought traps to increasing self-esteem, controlling anger, and developing resilience, this workbook has taught you a lot. You've learned effective methods and instruments to comprehend your feelings, ideas, and actions. However, CBT takes time to master, just like learning a new skill like playing an instrument or participating in sports. It requires perseverance, practice, and a dedication to incorporating it into your life. In order to continue growing, thriving, and living your best life.

This chapter focuses on maintaining your momentum by incorporating CBT into your everyday activities. Making these beneficial adjustments last is the goal!

Let's consider a situation that is comparable. Let's say you have acquired the skill of riding a bicycle. You've worked on steering, pedaling, and balancing. You may now ride with assurance. However, if you take a long break from riding, you may feel a little unsteady when you resume.

In a similar vein, you may find it more difficult to apply CBT skills when you need them if you stop practicing them. CBT is a skill set, and like all skills, it needs constant practice to be strong. It's a process of self-discovery and personal development rather than a quick remedy. CBT will become more automatic and natural the more you include it into your everyday routine.

**The following are some methods to incorporate CBT into your life:**

- **Cultivate the habit**: Try to make CBT exercises a part of your everyday routine, much like you would with your homework or teeth. Every day, set aside some time to ponder about your ideas, confront bad thoughts, or engage in a relaxing exercise. Make use of visual cues: Sticky notes with coping mechanisms or positive affirmations should be placed in areas you'll see frequently, such as your desk, locker, or mirror. You can maintain awareness of your CBT abilities with the aid of these visual reminders.

- **Maintain a journal**: Journaling can be an effective way to measure your progress and reflect on yourself. Jot down bad ideas or challenging feelings, your reaction to them, and the lessons you took away from the experience.

- **Look for a CBT partner**: Make contact with a friend, relative, or therapist who is knowledgeable with cognitive behavioral therapy. You may encourage one another, offer advice, and support one another.

- **Treat yourself with kindness and patience:** Don't expect to be flawless. Everyone makes mistakes from time to time. Do not give up if you discover that you are reverting to your previous habits. Simply return to your CBT exercises with gentleness.

- **Honor your accomplishments**: Recognize and honor your advancements, no matter how minor. This will support constructive improvements and keep you motivated.

- **Customize and modify**: There is no one-size-fits-all method for CBT. Try a variety of methods and approaches to see what suits you the best. Don't hesitate to modify the tools to suit your own requirements and tastes.

- **Make it enjoyable**: It is not necessary for CBT to be solemn or dull. Look for methods to make it fun. To examine your thoughts and feelings, engage in creative pursuits such as writing, music, or sketching.

Let's examine some actual instances of how children and teenagers might apply CBT in their daily lives: Consider Alex, a student who has learnt how to confront his negative self-talk. He could develop the practice of taking a few minutes every day to examine his thoughts and spot any unfavorable thought patterns. To remind himself of his strengths, he may also attach sticky notes with encouraging quotes on his mirror.

Here's another illustration: Consider Sarah, a teenager who has mastered the art of controlling her rage. She may record the things that make her angry and her reactions in a journal. She may also assemble a "coping skills toolbox" with calming tools, such as a relaxation CD or a stress ball.

Try this enjoyable hobby: Assign yourself a "CBT Challenge" Decide which CBT skill or skills you want to concentrate on, then make it your mission to practice them consistently for a week. Keep track of your progress and treat yourself when you reach your objective.

Teaching someone else about CBT is another action you can attempt. You can strengthen your own comprehension and increase the automaticity of the skills by explaining the ideas and methods to another person.

Keep in mind that incorporating CBT into your life is a process rather than a final goal. It involves always learning new things and improving your abilities. It's about giving oneself the ability to take charge of your ideas, emotions, and actions in order to lead a more contented, joyful, and healthy life.

Maintaining CBT can help you develop resilience, overcome obstacles in life, and realize your full potential. Well done for making this significant move in the direction of a better future!

## Creating a CBT Toolkit: Your Go-To Resources

*"Give me six hours to chop down a tree and I will spend the first four sharpening the axe."* – Abraham Lincoln

Consider yourself a carpenter who is going to construct a home. Without your instruments, you wouldn't begin, would you? Along with other necessary tools, you would need your hammer, saw, and measuring tape. In a similar vein, you need the appropriate skills to manage your thoughts, feelings, and behaviors.

The focus of this subchapter is on building your own customized CBT toolkit, which is a set of tools and techniques you can use anytime you need a little more help. It's similar to creating your own first aid kit for your mind!

Let's consider a situation that is comparable. Consider yourself extremely nervous about a presentation you have to give at school. You have sweaty palms, a pounding heart, and pessimistic thoughts like "What if I mess up?""What if everyone laughs at me?" In times like these, having a CBT toolkit on hand can be immensely beneficial.

You can manage your thoughts, feelings, and behaviors with the help of the tools and techniques in your CBT toolkit. It's a customized set of methods you've acquired throughout this workbook, made to fit your unique requirements and tastes. It's similar to having a reliable buddy or counselor by your side at all times to provide support and direction.

**You could add the following elements to your CBT toolkit**:

- **Affirmations That Are Positive**: You can tell yourself these affirmations on a daily basis, particularly when you're having trouble thinking positively. Examples include: "I am capable,""I am strong,""I am worthy."

- **Records of Thought**: These are diary entries or worksheets that assist you in recognizing, disputing, and reframing negative ideas. They offer a methodical approach to analyzing the arguments for and against your ideas and creating more impartial viewpoints.

- **Relaxation Methods**: These techniques, which include progressive muscle relaxation, mindfulness meditation, deep breathing exercises, and visualization, can help you deal with stress and anxiety.

- **Coping Techniques**: These are coping mechanisms you employ when faced with uncomfortable feelings or circumstances. Examples include journaling, exercising, talking to a friend, taking up a hobby, or spending time outdoors.

- **Methods for Setting Goals**: These are methods for tracking your progress, breaking down big goals into smaller ones, and creating realistic and attainable goals.

- **List of Positive Attributes and Strengths**: Here is a list of your strong points, abilities, and skills. During difficult circumstances, going over this list can help you remember your strengths and increase your sense of self-worth.

- **Inspiring Phrases or Pictures**: These are sayings or pictures that uplift, encourage, or cheer you up. Keep them close at hand for an instant mood lift. Include the phone numbers or email addresses of dependable family members, friends, therapists, or support hotlines so that you can get in touch with them in case you need assistance.

- **Nature Sounds or Relaxing Music**: One useful strategy for reducing tension and anxiety is to listen to relaxing music or natural noises.

Fidget toys, such as a stress ball, can assist manage anxiety and relieve physical tension.

Let's examine some actual instances of how children and teenagers can apply their CBT toolkits:

Consider Alex, a student who feels overburdened by his coursework. To handle his stress, he may utilize his CBT toolkit to make a study timetable, divide up big assignments into smaller ones, and engage in deep breathing techniques.

Here's another illustration: Consider Sarah, a teenager who is self-conscious about the way she looks. She might practice self-compassion, confront negative self-talk, and go over her list of positive traits and strengths using her CBT tools.

Try this enjoyable hobby: Make a tangible CBT toolset. Locate a container, bag, or box and embellish it. Fill it with objects that symbolize the CBT techniques and materials you have selected. This might be a stress ball, relaxation CDs, thinking journal worksheets, printed versions of positive affirmations, or anything else you find useful.

Making a digital CBT toolset is an additional task you could attempt. Make a folder on your phone or computer where you may keep digital copies of your CBT materials, like links to useful websites, guided meditations, relaxation music, and positive affirmations.

Keep in mind that your CBT toolkit is a personal resource that you can alter to suit your own requirements and tastes. It's a set of resources that can help you control your ideas, emotions, and actions as well as face life's obstacles with more resilience and self-assurance.

You'll be better able to manage stress, get beyond challenges, and have a happier, healthier, and more satisfying life if you consistently use the tools in your toolkit. We'll examine some more resources that can help you on your continuous path of self-discovery and development in the upcoming

## CELEBRATING YOUR PROGRESS:

## RECOGNIZING YOUR GROWTH

*"Progress is not achieved by doing extraordinary things. It is achieved by doing ordinary things with extraordinary consistency."* – Mother Teresa

Consider picking up a new skill, such as playing a sport or an instrument. Being a master overnight is not what you would anticipate, would it? It requires commitment, practice, and time. Learning and using CBT skills is no different. It's a path of personal development, and it's critical to acknowledge and appreciate your accomplishments as you go.

Giving yourself credit for all of your incredible work, appreciating your progress, and recognizing your efforts are the main topics of this subchapter. Now is the moment to honor YOU!

Let's consider a situation that is comparable. Let's say you have been practicing anger management. You used to lose your temper quickly, but now you can calmly express your feelings, take a deep breath, and count to 10. This is a MASSIVE achievement! It's an indication that your efforts are having an impact, and it should be honored.

Maintaining motivation and growing requires acknowledging your accomplishments. It gives you a sense of accomplishment, validates your progress, and increases your self-assurance in your capacity to overcome obstacles. It serves as a reminder that you're headed in the correct path even if you haven't arrived at your destination yet, much like consulting a map throughout a lengthy travel.

However, it might be simple to ignore our advancements at times. Instead of recognizing how much we've accomplished so far, we can concentrate more on the areas where we still need to improve. Because of this, it's critical to intentionally recognize our progress, no matter how modest.

**The following techniques will help you identify your progress:**

- **Maintain a journal**: Write down your experiences on a regular basis, highlighting instances in which you successfully applied your CBT techniques. Consider how you overcame obstacles in a different way than you might have in the past. This can assist you in recognizing trends in your development and pinpointing areas in which you've advanced significantly.

- **Monitor your progress**: To monitor your progress toward your objectives, use graphs, charts, and other visual aids. You may, for instance, keep a chart that records how many negative ideas you have every day if you're trying to cut back on your negative self-talk. You'll be able to see concrete proof of your success as the number drops.

- **Appreciate minor triumphs:** Don't only concentrate on the major achievements. Celebrate and acknowledge your little victories along the road. Have you been able to maintain your composure under pressure? Did you confront a pessimistic notion and swap it out for a constructive one? These minor triumphs hold equal significance to the more significant ones.

- **Request feedback**: Ask therapists, family members, or close friends what they think about your development. They might see improvements that you haven't noticed yourself.

- **Give yourself a reward**: Give yourself something you like when you reach a goal or make great strides. This will help you stay motivated and reinforce good conduct.

- **Consider your journey**: Spend some time thinking back on your personal development and self-discovery path. Consider your progress, the obstacles you've surmounted, and the abilities you've acquired. Take pride in all of your hard work.

Let's examine some actual instances of how children and teenagers can identify their development:

Consider Alex, a student who has been attempting to control his test anxiety. Before tests, he used to become so anxious that he would freeze and lose his ability to think.

However, he's since learnt to control his anxiousness by using deep breathing exercises and constructive self-talk. He observes that his grades have increased and that he can concentrate better on tests. He ought to rejoice because this is an obvious indication of advancement.

Here's another illustration: Consider Sarah, a teenager who has been attempting to improve her sense of self-worth. She used to constantly compare herself to other people and be quite critical of herself.

She has since learnt to emphasize her positive traits and strengths, though. She observes that her confidence has increased and that she is more open to trying new things. She ought to recognize and appreciate this important advancement.

Try this enjoyable hobby: Construct a "Progress Jar." Decorate a jar and set it somewhere that others can see it. Write down your accomplishments on a slip of paper and place it in the jar as you make progress in your CBT journey. To remind yourself of your progress, pull out a couple slips of paper and read them whenever you're feeling down.

Another task you could attempt is making a "Timeline of Growth." Make a timeline and highlight significant turning points in your CBT journey. Mention both significant and minor achievements. This graphic depiction of your development can serve as a potent reminder of your development and fortitude.

Recall that acknowledging your success is a crucial component of the cognitive behavioral therapy process. It supports your continued growth, confidence-building, and motivation.

It's about honoring the fantastic person you are becoming and recognizing all the amazing work you have done. You'll be well-prepared to carry on with your self-discovery journey and lead a happier, healthier, and more satisfying life if you acknowledge your progress.

## SELF-REFLECTION QUESTIONS

1. How have you used CBT skills in your daily life so far?

   _____

   _____

   _____

2. What CBT techniques do you find most helpful?

   _____

   _____

   _____

3. What are some challenges you face in keeping up with your CBT practice?

   _____

   _____

   _____

4. How can you make CBT a more regular part of your routine?

   _____

   _____

   _____

5. How will you know when you've made progress in your CBT journey? What are your measures of success?

_____

_____

_____

## TRANSFORMATIVE EXERCISES

1. "CBT Habit Tracker": Create a chart or calendar to track your daily or weekly CBT practice. Include activities like challenging negative thoughts, practicing calming techniques, or using thought records. Check off each activity as you complete it.

2. "CBT Toolkit Creation": Gather or create resources that you find helpful for your CBT practice. This could include positive affirmations, thought record worksheets, relaxation scripts, journal prompts, or contact information for support. Keep these resources in a designated place (physical or digital) for easy access.

3. "Progress Journal": Regularly write about situations where you used CBT skills effectively. Describe the situation, what you did differently, and the positive outcome. This helps you see your growth over time.

4. "CBT Buddy System": Find a friend, family member, or therapist who is also familiar with CBT. Support each other by sharing tips, discussing challenges, and celebrating successes.

5. "Personalized CBT Plan": Develop a personalized plan for integrating CBT into your life. Identify specific CBT strategies you want to focus on, how often you will practice them, and how you will track your progress. Make this plan realistic and achievable for your lifestyle.

# CHAPTER TWELVE

## SEEK HELP

---

*"It takes courage to ask for help when you need it. Don't be afraid to reach out."* – Unknown

You've gained a lot of knowledge about controlling your emotions, ideas, and actions. You've improved your coping mechanisms, problem-solving techniques, and resilience. You have an amazing arsenal of tactics at your disposal. However, even the most experienced builders occasionally require the advice of an architect, and even the most courageous adventurers occasionally require a guide.

This chapter focuses on identifying when you may require further assistance and knowing how to ask specialists and mature adults for it. It's about understanding that seeking assistance is a show of strength rather than weakness.

Let's consider a situation that is comparable. Consider yourself learning a new sport. You're improving because you've watched videos and practiced the fundamentals. However, you're still having trouble with a specific method. You could continue practicing alone in the hopes of learning it eventually. Alternatively, you might seek assistance from a coach or a more seasoned athlete. You can learn more quickly and handle challenges more skillfully if you ask an expert for advice.

In a similar vein, there are instances in which getting professional assistance might improve your mental and emotional health. It's not about recognizing a weakness or conceding defeat. It's about realizing that in order to handle the challenges of life, we occasionally require additional assistance.

**Here are a few indicators that it may be time to get more assistance**:

- **Your difficulties are ongoing**: It could be time to get professional help if you've been dealing with a certain problem for a while and your go-to coping mechanisms aren't working. For instance, it's crucial to speak with someone if you've been dealing with ongoing depressive or anxious sensations that are interfering with your day-to-day activities.

- **Your difficulties are severe**: Seeking expert assistance is essential if you're dealing with really strong emotions that are hard to control, such severe anxiety, panic attacks, or uncontrollable rage.

- **Your life is being impacted by your challenges**: It's time to get treatment if your relationships, academic performance, sleep patterns, or general quality of life is being negatively impacted by your mental or emotional health.

- Seeking support is crucial, for instance, if your anxiety is causing you to avoid social situations or if your fears are making it difficult for you to focus in class.

- **A major event in your life has occurred**: Navigating significant life transitions, like losing a loved one, moving with family, or going through a terrible event, may be extremely difficult. During these moments, getting expert assistance can offer helpful support and direction.

- **You're considering hurting yourself or other people**: It's critical that you get help right away if you're thinking about hurting yourself or other people. These are significant ideas that shouldn't be disregarded. Speak with a responsible adult or give a crisis hotline a call.

**Who can you ask for more assistance**?

- **Guardians or parents**: The first people you can turn to for support are frequently your parents or guardians. They want the best for you because they love you.

- **Other responsible adults**: You can talk to a trusted adult, like a grandparent, an aunt or uncle, a teacher, a coach, or a school counselor, if you don't feel comfortable talking to your parents.

- **A school psychologist or counselor**: Psychologists and school counselors are qualified experts who may offer help and direction on a variety of topics, such as relationship challenges, stress, anxiety, depression, and bullying.

- **Counselor or therapist**: Counselors and therapists are mental health specialists who can offer family or individual therapy. They can assist you in comprehending your difficulties, acquiring coping mechanisms, and processing challenging feelings.

- **Doctor**: For assistance with mental health, your doctor can also be a great resource. If required, they can evaluate your needs and recommend you to other experts.

It's critical to keep in mind that asking for assistance is a show of strength rather than weakness. Recognizing that you need help and asking for it requires bravery. You're taking care of your mental and emotional health and giving yourself the tools you need to live a happier and better life by asking professionals and mature adults for help.

## PARENTS AND CAREGIVERS SECTION

You are essential in promoting your child's mental and emotional health as parents and other caregivers.

**You can assist in the following ways:**

- **Establish a secure and encouraging environment**: Give your youngster the confidence to talk to you about anything without worrying about being judged. Establish an environment where people can freely express their emotions.

- **Pay attention**: Observe how your child acts and how they are feeling. Keep an eye out for alterations in their social interactions, eating, sleep habits, or mood. These might indicate that they're having difficulties.

- **Pay close attention**: When your child speaks to you, pay close attention and show empathy. Make an effort to comprehend their viewpoint and respect their emotions.

- **Provide encouragement and support**: Express to your child your belief in their capacity to overcome obstacles and your support.

- **Ask for expert assistance as necessary**: If you are worried about your child's mental or emotional health, don't be afraid to get expert assistance. The impact of early intervention can be significant.

- **Educate yourself on the mental health of children and adolescents**. You will be better able to comprehend your child's requirements and offer the right kind of support as a result.

- **Look after you**: Being a parent may be difficult. To be the finest support system for your child, make sure you're looking after your own mental and emotional well. Remind yourself that you are not alone. You and your child can get support from a variety of places. Together, you can assist your child in acquiring the coping mechanisms and resilience necessary for success.

# CONCLUSION

You've arrived at the conclusion of our adventure together, a voyage of self-discovery and empowerment through the terrain of your own mind. You've learnt to confront negative thinking, you've investigated the power of your thoughts, and you've realized how strong you are.

You've improved your problem-solving abilities, strengthened your resilience, and created coping mechanisms for your emotions. You've learned to appreciate your accomplishments, identified your special strengths, and realized the value of self-compassion.

You've even learned how and when to ask for help, understanding that doing so shows courage rather than weakness. Well done! You've given yourself a set of abilities and tactics that will benefit you for the rest of your life.

This isn't the "end", though, is it? It's more like the start. Consider this book as a starting point rather than a final destination. You now understand the foundational ideas of cognitive behavioral therapy.

It is now your responsibility to use these ideas and incorporate them into your everyday routine. Like learning a new language, it will take time to become proficient. It requires constant work, practice, and the ability to be patient with oneself. There will be moments when you make a mistake, when unpleasant ideas resurface, or when you find it difficult to control your emotions. That is quite typical. Everything is a part of the process. The key is to continue honing your skills and utilizing the resources you've learned, and to keep believing in your ability to grow and change.

Consider your mind to be a garden. There may occasionally be weeds of negative thinking, but you now know how to spot them, pluck them out by their roots, and plant a garden of self-compassion and positive thinking.

Just as maintaining a plant requires constant care and attention, so too does maintaining your mental and emotional health. A few weeds may emerge, but don't give up. The lovely flowers of resilience, self-assurance, and delight will bloom and grow if you simply continue to care for your garden and your mind.

Keep in mind that this is "your" journey. These concepts can be applied in any fashion; there is no right or wrong approach. Try out a variety of methods, determine which suits you best, and modify the resources to suit your own requirements and situation.

Don't be scared to customize your strategy and come up with your own special combination of tactics that will enable you to live your greatest life. Additionally, keep in mind that you are not traveling alone.

Your network of friends, family, mentors, teachers, and possibly even a therapist are there to support you, cheer you on, and help you celebrate your accomplishments. When you need a little more help, don't be afraid to ask for it. Everybody needs assistance occasionally, and asking for assistance is a show of strength not weakness.

As you proceed, keep in mind your inner strength. You have the power to control your emotions, mold your thoughts, and design a meaningful, purposeful existence. You possess the fortitude to overcome obstacles, the bravery to confront your anxieties, and the discernment to acknowledge your own value. You deserve to be happy and healthy since you are strong and capable.

The voyage itself is yours to take, but this book has given you a map and a compass. Accept the journey, go into your inner world, and uncover the amazing potential that is inside of you. Continue to grow, practice, and have faith in your amazing self. The world is eager to witness your incredible abilities. Now shine brightly out there!

# Positive affirmations, kids can engage with, categorized for easier selection and tailored to the themes covered in the CBT workbook:

**General Self-Esteem & Confidence**:

- I believe in myself.
- I am capable of amazing things.
- I am strong and resilient.
- I am worthy of love and respect.
- I am unique and special.
- I am learning and growing every day.
- I am proud of who I am.
- I accept myself, flaws and all.
- I am getting better at things all the time.
- I choose to be kind to myself.
- I am brave and can try new things.
- I trust myself to make good decisions.
- I am getting stronger every day.
- I am enough, just as I am.
- I celebrate my successes, big and small.

## Managing Thoughts & Feelings:

- My thoughts are just thoughts, they are not always true.
- I can choose to think positive thoughts.
- I am in control of my feelings.
- I can learn to manage my anger.
- It's okay to feel all my feelings.
- I can handle difficult situations.
- I can calm myself down when I'm stressed.
- I am learning to understand my emotions.
- I can choose how I react to things.
- I am getting better at managing my feelings.
- I can ask for help when I need it.
- I am strong and can get through tough times.
- I am learning and growing from my experiences.
- I can choose to be happy.
- I am getting better at understanding myself.

## Resilience & Problem-Solving:

- I can bounce back from challenges.
- I learn from my mistakes.
- I am resourceful and can find solutions.

- I am persistent and don't give up easily.
- I can overcome obstacles.
- I am getting better at solving problems.
- I am stronger than I think.
- I can handle whatever comes my way.
- I am growing more resilient every day.
- I can ask for help when I need it.
- I am brave and can face my fears.
- I am learning and growing from every experience.
- I can choose to be positive.
- I am capable of achieving my goals.
- I am getting better at learning from my mistakes.

## Using the Affirmations:

- Repetition: Encourage kids to repeat the affirmations regularly, either aloud or silently in their minds.
- Visualization: Suggest they imagine themselves embodying the affirmation, feeling the confidence or calmness it describes.
- Personalization: Encourage kids to adapt the affirmations to make them more personal and meaningful to them.

- Writing: Have them write the affirmations down, perhaps in a journal or on sticky notes placed where they will see them often.

## A NOTE OF GRATITUDE

Dear Reader,

As you hold this book in your hands, I want to express my sincere gratitude for your support. It is with immense joy and humility that I share these words with you, hoping they will resonate with you on your journey towards a more peaceful and fulfilling life.

Writing this book has been a deeply personal and rewarding experience. My hope is that the insights, strategies, and practices shared within these pages will provide you with the tools and support you need to overcome these challenges with greater ease and grace.

Your decision to purchase this book is a testament to your commitment to personal growth and well-being. I am truly honored to be a part of your journey.
If this book has resonated with you, I encourage you to:

Share it with others: If you know someone who might benefit from this book, please consider sharing the knowledge or better still encourage them to get theirs and more importantly make **positive review** on lesson learnt from this book. You could make a significant difference in their lives.

Thank you again for your support. I wish you all the best on your path to a life filled with peace, joy, and fulfillment.

With heartfelt gratitude,

John H. Eric

Made in the USA
Monee, IL
06 May 2025